First published in the United States of America
by Fair Winds Press
33 Commercial Street
Gloucester, Massachusetts 01930-5089
Telephone: 978-282-9590
Facsimile: 978-283-2742

ISBN 1-931412-50-2

10 9 8 7 6 5 4 3 2 1

Pinted in China

♥

Dedicated to my Grandpa
Robert Paul Hinton~

When I was a little girl my Grandpa Bob's talent for oil painting and sculpture amazed me. It seems he was always doing pencil drawings for me to color in or working on another masterpiece. The most beautiful card I ever received was one he made for me with chickens and a palm tree on the front.

He grew up in Southern Minnesota and later moved to Florida with my Grandma Helen.

When I was 8 years old I was lucky enough to be able to travel with my mom, dad, brothers and aunt to visit my grandparents. I'll never forget that summer! I'll never forget how Grandpa made sculptures in the white beach sand, made crabcakes in their little kitchen, and found some of the prettiest seashells I've ever laid eyes on. I'll never forget his warm laugh, how his eyes danced when he was teasing us kids, and I'll never forget the man that encouraged me to be creative. He inspires me to this day.

Contents

A. M. LINDBERGH

"Women need solitude in order to find again the true essence of themselves."

Spa recipe Essentials

Blender
Cutting Board
Eyedropper
Funnels in assorted sizes
Bowls
Gloves
Grater
Measuring Cups
Measuring Spoons
Mortar & Pestle
Sharp Knives
Pans
Rubber Spatula
Coffee Grinder
Wooden Spoons
Strainer
Metal Tongs
Carrot Peeler
Assorted Jars
Tins
Muslin & assorted Fabrics
Sewing Machine
String, Twine & Ribbon
Small Wire Whisk
Bottles with Corks
Rubber Gloves

Microwave
Cheesecloth
Paper Towels
Spray Bottles
Soap Moulds
Waxed paper

NOTE: Once you have used a cooking utensil for a spa recipe, don't use it for food preparation. Also, avoid using pans & tools that contain copper, cast iron or aluminum. These metals may react badly to some of the ingredients in your spa recipes.

"Oh, thou art fairer than the evening air clad in the beauty of a thousand stars."

~ Marlowe

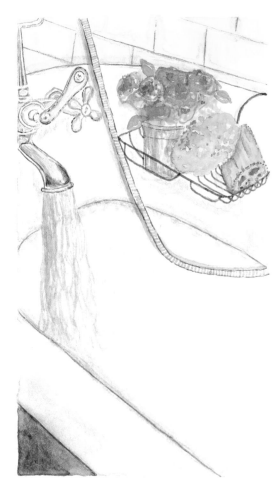

Little Luxuries ♥
For Your Bathtime

- A little table to keep next to your tub for books, violet scented bath beads, Victoria Magazines, a cup of chamomile tea, a bud vase and maybe a chocolate truffle ☺
- A few drops of sandalwood oil in your bath will transport you to exotic lands.
- Set a garden trellis or a piece of lattice in your bathroom and decorate it with stems of silk wisteria.
- Keep your soaps, gels, lotions & shampoos in a big galvanized watering can.
- Decorate your bathroom in a seaside theme. Use fishnets, shells, starfish, lighthouse & boat decorations.
- Ivy plants will thrive in the bathroom. The moisture and lights create a greenhouse atmosphere.
- Roll hand towels and put them in a small metal wine rack.
- Paint clouds on your ceiling.
- Hang fairy lights around your mirror.
- Cucumber slices on your eyelids.
- Listen to a book on tape while you soak.
- Hide the pipes under a sink with a pretty sink skirt on a velcro strip.
- A terrycloth covered bath tub pillow.
- A blue lightbulb in place of a white one.

"What is elegance? Soap & water!" ♥

Cecil Beaton ♥

2

"There must be quite a few things a hot bath won't cure, but I don't know many of them."
• Sylvia Plath

3

The Enchanted Bath

"*I adore simple pleasures. They are the last refuge of the complex*"
— OSCAR WILDE

EXFOLIATING SALT
TREATMENT

This is a soothing, cleansing body treatment that will leave your skin feeling baby soft and refreshed!

In a medium glass mixing bowl, combine:

4 cups de-iodized salt
1/4 cup baby oil
1 cup purified water

Wet entire body by taking a quick warm shower. Turn off water. Scoop out a handful of salt mixture & rub onto skin in a gentle circular motion. Add more mixture as needed. Be sure to avoid face and genital areas. Rinse. Wash with a rough, soapy washcloth. Rinse. Wait 2 hours before using a moisturizer. Avoid open sores & Varicose Veins.

"I have bathed in the Poem of the Sea..." ARTHUR RIMBAUD

Rose Petal Dream Bath

Imagine bathing in a warm pool in the middle of your own secret rose garden. To make the dream come true, add 1 Tablespoon of each of the following herbs to a small muslin bag:

- Lavender
- Rosemary
- Camomile
- Lemon Balm
- + 2 Tablespoons Oatmeal
- & 2 Tablespoons Green Tea

Tie bag tightly closed with a ribbon & hang under bathtub faucet as the tub is filling. Just before you step into the tub, add 2 cups fresh rose petals to bath water.

"Gather ye rosebuds while ye may, Old Time is still a-flying: And this same flower that smiles to-day, To-morrow will be dying."

Robert Herrick

6

Soothing Lemon Soak

When life gives you lemons... Indulge in a wonderful lemon bath! It's easy! Just slice a lemon into a tub of warm water and hop in! Soaking in a lemon bath is relaxing, and the healing oils in lemon peel will sooth sunburned skin.

For shiny, smooth hair — Squeeze the juice of one lemon into a liquid measuring cup & pour over hair. Rinse. ♥

7

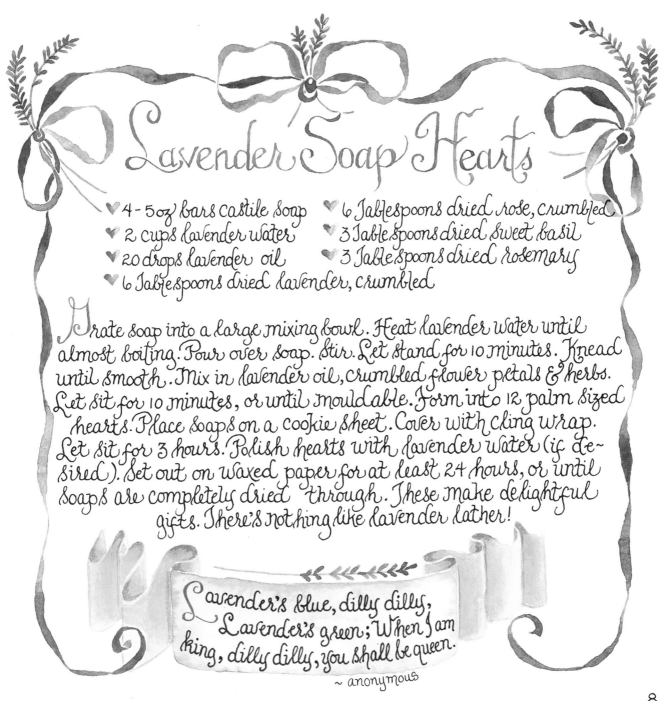

Lavender Soap Hearts

- ♥ 4 - 5 oz bars Castile Soap
- ♥ 2 cups lavender water
- ♥ 20 drops lavender oil
- ♥ 6 Tablespoons dried lavender, crumbled
- ♥ 6 Tablespoons dried rose, crumbled
- ♥ 3 Tablespoons dried sweet basil
- ♥ 3 Tablespoons dried rosemary

Grate soap into a large mixing bowl. Heat lavender water until almost boiling. Pour over soap. Stir. Let stand for 10 minutes. Knead until smooth. Mix in lavender oil, crumbled flower petals & herbs. Let sit for 10 minutes, or until mouldable. Form into 12 palm sized hearts. Place soaps on a cookie sheet. Cover with cling wrap. Let sit for 3 hours. Polish hearts with lavender water (if desired). Set out on waxed paper for at least 24 hours, or until soaps are completely dried through. These make delightful gifts. There's nothing like lavender lather!

Lavender's blue, dilly dilly,
Lavender's green; When I am
king, dilly dilly, you shall be queen.

~ anonymous

8

Classic Oatmeal Soap

A BEAUTIFULLY SCENTED VERSION OF THE CLASSIC OATMEAL SOAP! ENJOY...

8 teaspoons caustic soda
1 pint purified water
4 Tablespoons vanilla oil
4 Tablespoons coconut oil
4 Tablespoons glycerine
4 teaspoons wildflower honey
5 drops sandalwood oil
2 drops patchouli oil
1/4 cup coarsely ground oatmeal

Use your imagination when choosing moulds for your soaps. Above all, have fun! ♥

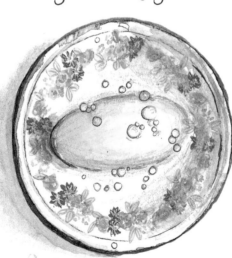

Decorate the completed, waxed paper wrapped bars with raffia, ribbon, or twine bows... or whatever your heart desires!

POUR water into a large glass bowl. Wearing rubber gloves to protect your hands, stir soda into water until completely dissolved. In a saucepan mix vanilla oil, coconut oil, glycerine and honey over very low heat until warm. Working carefully and quickly, stir oil mixture into soda solution. Stirring constantly and vigorously, add sandalwood oil, patchouli oil and oatmeal. Stir until thick, smooth and white. Pour into moulds lined with cling wrap. Let sit for one or two days so the soap can set completely. Using saran wrap edges, remove soap from moulds. Peel off saran wrap. Wrap soap bars in waxed paper.

"There be none of beauty's daughters
With a Magic like thee;
And like music on the waters
Is thy sweet voice to me." Lord Byron

"IF I WERE A WOMAN, I'D WEAR

JOHN VAN DRUTEN...

COFFEE AS A PERFUME"

Coffee & Cream Soap

4 teaspoons coffee beans
1- 8 oz bar unscented glycerine soap
2 teaspoons heavy whipping cream
2 teaspoons aloe vera gel

Grind the coffee beans. Grate the glycerine soap, and melt it over low heat in a heavy sauce-pan. When soap is liquified, remove the pan from heat. Add coffee, cream & aloe. Mix well. Pour into moulds. Allow to set 3-4 hours. If you like coffee, you'll love this soap! Just like a warm cuppa joe in the morning, the scent of coffee & cream soap will invigorate your senses! Yum...

Hazelnut Coffee

CREAM

BEAUTY ADVICE FROM A MAN

LOVE POTION

Rose water

🌹 1½ cups Purified water

🌹 ⅛ cup Vodka

🌹 1 generous handful fresh rose petals

🌹 6 drops rose scented essential oil

Delicate and dreamy.   This "potion" will cause him to follow you around the house and give you flowers "just because."

In a decorative perfume bottle, combine water, vodka, and fresh rose petals. Seal tightly and shake gently. Store in a cool, dry place for 7 days. Strain out rose petals. Then add essential oil. Return to bottle and store in refrigerator. ♥ Wear on pulse points as a perfume. Use in any of my spa recipes that call for rose water ∴

"Perfumes, colors and sounds echo one another."
Charles Baudelaire

MILK BATH

Milk is rich in protein and fats that beautifully nourish and moisturize the skin. Soak in this particular milk bath for at least 20 minutes.

- 2/3 cup powdered milk
- 1/4 cup corn starch
- 1/4 cup honey
- 6 drops rose oil or 1/4 c. rosewater
- 1/4 c. water

Blend above ingredients in a blender. If rosewater is used in place of rose oil, the 1/4 cup regular water should be omitted. Add mixture to a full tub of water. Sprinkle 2 Tablespoons orange peel into your milk bath. Get in! :)

"Where are you going to, my pretty maid?" "I'm going a-milking, sir," she said.

ANONYMOUS NURSERY RHYME ♥

Effervescent Pink Champagne Bath

A SWEET LUXURY FOR YOUR SKIN...

add the following ingredients to a tub of warm water.

- 2 cups pink champagne
- 3 tablespoons of your favorite bubble bath
- 5 drops red food coloring
- 2 tablespoons baby oil
- ¼ cup rock salt crystals

light some candles, pour yourself a glass of champagne or juice, and enjoy!

"Toast love, life & happiness... Take a champagne bath... The very pink of perfection." Oliver Goldsmith

"The magic
of a face."

— Thomas Carew

Celebrating Natural Beauty. Treatments to pamper your...

FACE

"But Lancelot mused a little space; He said, "She has a lovely face; God in his mercy lend her grace, The Lady of Shallot."" ♥ Tennyson

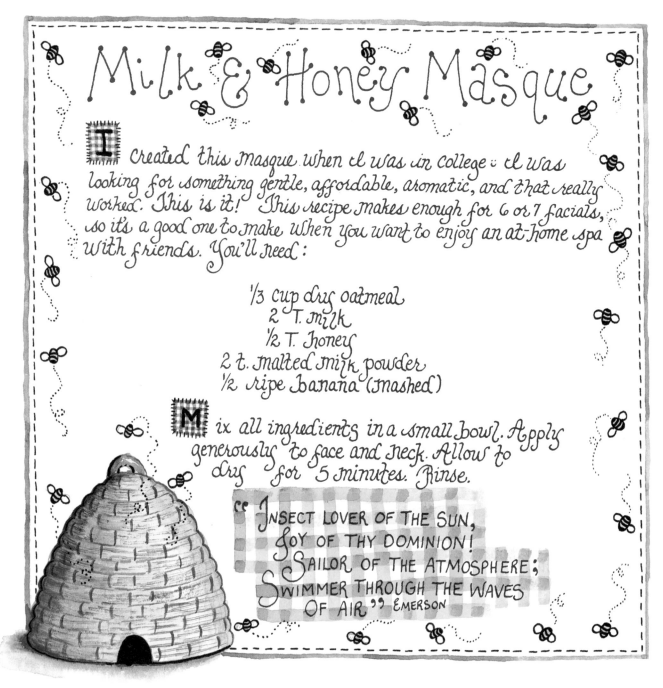

Milk & Honey Masque

I created this masque when I was in college. I was looking for something gentle, affordable, aromatic, and that really worked. This is it! This recipe makes enough for 6 or 7 facials, so it's a good one to make when you want to enjoy an at-home spa with friends. You'll need:

⅓ cup dry oatmeal
2 T. milk
½ T. honey
2 t. malted milk powder
½ ripe banana (mashed)

Mix all ingredients in a small bowl. Apply generously to face and neck. Allow to dry for 5 minutes. Rinse.

"Insect lover of the sun,
Joy of thy dominion!
Sailor of the atmosphere;
Swimmer through the waves
Of air." EMERSON

17

♥ Fancy 5 Step Pressure Point Facial

A fancy shmancy spa facial that will relax and renew. It moisturizes* dry skin & stimulates circulation. Prior to doing the facial, wash and tone your face. Using the middle finger of both hands, press the following pressure points using a gentle, firm touch. Do each point for 5 sec.

1. Inhale and press your forehead above the center of each eyebrow. Exhale as you release.

Repeat. Breathe deeply.

2. Inhale and press the outside corners of each eye near temples.

Exhale as you release.

Repeat.

3. Inhale and press the corners of your nose.

Exhale as you release.

Repeat. Feel the tension melting away.

4. Inhale and press the corners of your mouth.

Exhale as you release.

Repeat.

Picture ocean waves.

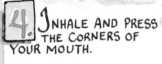
Fresh Fruit

5. Inhale and press the point just beneath your chin.

Exhale as you release.

Repeat. Take a nap ☺

*your favorite face moisturizer can be used for this facial if you wish.

Apricot Scrub
For a Radiant Complexion

Pure ambrosia! Mild & nourishing. The scent is addictive...

5 dried apricots
3 figs
⅓ c. buttermilk
1 T. aloe vera juice

a natural sponge is kind to skin...

5 drops vitamin E oil
½ tsp. bran flour
½ tsp. bee pollen
½ T. crushed almonds

Allow dried apricots & figs to soften in a cup of purified water for 45 minutes to an hour. Strain off water with a small sieve or strainer. Pour fruits and the rest of the wet ingredients into a blender. Puree. Add dry ingredients little by little. Puree. Use on face as a cleanser or as an all-over body scrub. Cover & refrigerate up to 5 days.

"It is astonishing how short a time it takes for very wonderful things to happen." FRANCES HODGSON BURNETT

Sweet Nothings Steamer

Like walking along a cobblestone street in London on a misty morning. Steam facials improve the circulation in your face & cause a beautiful, youthful glow!

Boil 2 quarts of water in a big pot. To boiling water add: ⅓ cup dried roses, ⅓ cup chamomile, & ⅓ cup dried rosemary. Cover and turn off heat. Let steep for 3 minutes. Uncover and transfer to a basin. Place basin on a table. Drape a bath towel over your head, and hold your face 6 to 12 inches over the water. Steam for 15 minutes. Wipe moisture droplets from your face with a washcloth. Tone with a little vodka applied to a cotton ball. (This will close & cool your pores.) Note: If you notice a slight, itchy sensation, it is just your circulation improving! ☺ With each steamer the itchy sensation should decrease. You can do a steamer once a week.

fountain of youth facials ★

Sweetie Pie Strawberry
Mix 10 mashed strawberries with 3 Tablespoons honey. Apply to clean face. Remove after 10 min.

Peaches & Cream Dream
Mix 1 mashed peach with 1/4 cup vanilla yogurt. Apply to clean face. Remove after 15 minutes.

Go Bananas!
Mix 1/2 mashed banana, 2 teaspoons real coconut milk and 2 Tablespoons cooked barley. Apply to clean face. Remove after 10 minutes.

Cool as a Cucumber
Mix 3 Tablespoons mashed cucumber, 3 Tablespoons mashed Cantaloupe, and 3 minced peppermint leaves (fresh). Apply to clean face. Remove after 10 min.

Queen Bee
Mix one egg white with 1 teaspoon honey. Apply to clean face. Remove after 10 minutes.

Butter Maple
Mix 2 Tablespoons real maple syrup+1 Tablespoon powdered buttermilk. Apply to clean face. Remove after 10 minutes.

Orange "Peel"
Pour 1/4 cup orange juice and 1/4 cup purified water into a small sauce pan. Heat over a low flame until warm. Add 1 packet gelatin (unflavored). Stir until dissolved. Cool in fridge for 30 minutes. Apply thin coat of orange "peel" to face. Allow to dry. Peel off. Rinse face with cold water.

"There is a garden in her face..." ~Campion

Your Memories On Paper

JOURNALING FOR DREAMERS

An important part of your spa regimen is relaxation. One of my favorite ways to relax is by journaling. Here are some ideas of how you can get started putting your thoughts on paper.

I like having different journals for different seasons & themes. Some examples include: New Year's Resolutions & dreams in the winter, short stories, memories of childhood & poems in the summer, nature walk sketches & garden layouts in the springtime & autumn (GET YOUR COLORED PENCILS READY!), and recipes & traditions for the holidays. Use your imagination and begin setting the stage for dreams!

Find a special sanctuary where you can be alone with your thoughts and plans, or retreat to a nearby beach, porch, or garden. Sip tea, start potpourri simmering, treat yourself to a bouquet of your favorite flowers and play relaxing music. Indulge your senses and let your pen be your guide to tranquility...

Spa Music

SHAKESPEARE "THIS MUSIC CREPT BY ME UPON THE WATERS, ALLAYING BOTH THEIR FURY, AND MY PASSION, WITH ITS SWEET AIR."

LISTENING TO SOOTHING MUSIC ON YOUR SPA DAY CAN SET A RELAXED AND ROMANTIC MOOD. THE FOLLOWING SELECTIONS ARE SOME OF MY FAVORITES.

♪ Enya
♪ Rob Whitesides Woo
♪ Mozart
♪ Danny Wright
♪ The London Symphony Orchestra
♪ "The Bridges of Madison County" Soundtrack
♪ Loreena McKennitt
♪ CDs with nature sounds

♪ Billie Holiday - "Love Songs"
♪ Hallmark's "A Relaxing Soak in the Tub - Calming Classical Music"
♪ Billy McLaughlin - "Fingerdance"
♪ Beth Nielsen Chapman - "Sand and Water"
♪ Chopin
♪ Bach

"The horns of elfland faintly blowing, - Tennyson

"And the night shall be filled with music..." Henry Wadsworth Longfellow

Natural Miracles For Your Hair

"Oh, Brignal banks are wild and fair,
And Greta woods are green,
And you may gather garlands there
Would grace a summer queen."
SIR WALTER SCOTT

Thy baths shall
be the juice of
July-flowers, Spirit
of Roses, and of
Violets, The milk of
unicorns, and panther's
breath, gathered in bags,
and mixed with Cretan wines.

Ben Jonson

25

Jojoba Pomade

Deep conditioning treatments are especially needed for permed, colored, & heat styled hair. Try to get your hair trimmed regularly, and use your jojoba Pomade once a week.

To create Jojoba Pomade: In the top of a double boiler, heat 1 cup of purified water. When water is warm, add 2 teaspoons jojoba oil and 1 teaspoon vitamin E oil. Pour into a blender, and add 8 drops tea tree essential oil. Blend for 2 minutes.

To use: Wet hair. Pour pomade on hair. Work into hair & scalp. Add a little extra to dry ends. Leave in hair 10 minutes. Rinse thoroughly using cool water.

"For a breeze of morning moves,
And the planet of love is on high,
Beginning to faint in the light that she loves
On a bed of daffodil sky." —Tennyson

Spring Rain Vinegar Rinse & Purifier

Wash away shampoo residue with purifying vinegar. This will bring out the natural highlights and natural shine in your hair.

To make: Simply mix ½ cup white vinegar with ½ cup rain water. Cover and shake to mix. Shampoo & rinse as usual. Pour vinegar rinse over hair & massage into scalp. Condition as usual. Rinse with cool water.

"I WALKED FAR DOWN THE BEACH,
SOOTHED BY THE RHYTHM OF THE WAVES,...
THE WIND & MIST
FROM THE SPRAY ON MY HAIR."
·ANNE MORROW LINDBERGH

27

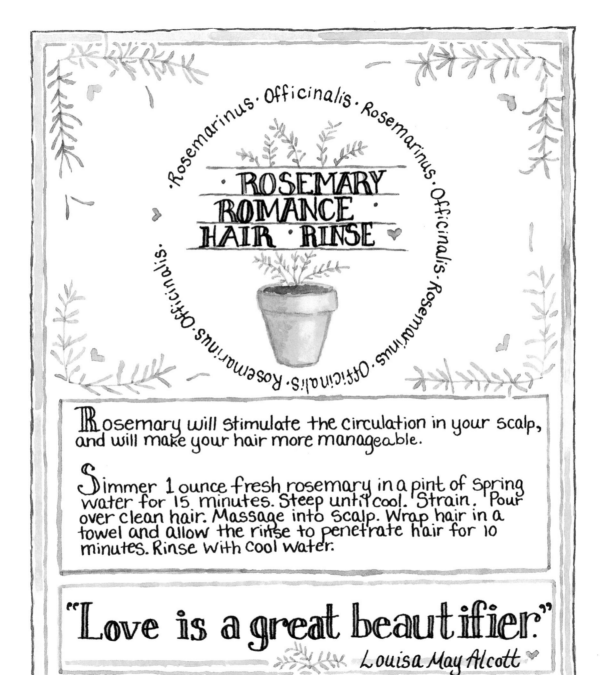

· ROSEMARY · ROMANCE · HAIR · RINSE ·

Rosemarinus · Officinalis · Rosemarinus · Officinalis · Rosemarinus · Officinalis · Rosemarinus · Officinalis ·

Rosemary will stimulate the circulation in your scalp, and will make your hair more manageable.

Simmer 1 ounce fresh rosemary in a pint of spring water for 15 minutes. Steep until cool. Strain. Pour over clean hair. Massage into scalp. Wrap hair in a towel and allow the rinse to penetrate hair for 10 minutes. Rinse with cool water.

"Love is a great beautifier."
Louisa May Alcott

28

OTHER NAMES FOR THE DANDELION... BLOW BALLS, NOON-HEAD-CLOCKS, MONK'S HEAD, & PRIEST'S CROWN

Dandelion Shampoo

BLOW ALL THE SEEDLINGS OFF IN ONE BREATH AND A WISH WILL BE GRANTED

DANDELION BLOSSOMS WILL NOURISH AND RESTORE BALANCE TO NORMAL HAIR. TO CREATE DANDELION SHAMPOO YOU WILL NEED...

- ❈ 4 TABLESPOONS BABY SHAMPOO
- ❈ 2 CUPS PURIFIED WATER
- ❈ ½ CUP FRESH DANDELION HEADS
- ❈ ½ TABLESPOON CHERRY BARK
- ❈ ½ TABLESPOON SPEARMINT LEAVES
- ❈ 2 TEASPOONS OLIVE OIL
- ❈ 5 DROPS GRAPEFRUIT ESSENTIAL OIL

PUT DANDELION HEADS IN A 20 OUNCE CANNING JAR. BOIL WATER AND POUR OVER DANDELION HEADS. COVER JAR WITH LID AND ALLOW TO STEEP FOR 15 MINUTES. ADD CHERRY BARK AND SPEARMINT TO JAR. COVER AND ALLOW TO STEEP FOR AN ADDITIONAL 10 MINUTES. STRAIN. RESERVE LIQUID. USING A FUNNEL, POUR THE SHAMPOO & DANDELION LIQUID INTO A PRETTY BOTTLE OR BACK INTO THE CANNING JAR. ADD OLIVE OIL AND ESSENTIAL OIL. SHAKE GENTLY TO COMBINE BEFORE EACH USE.

Shampooing Tips:

❈ ONLY A SMALL AMOUNT OF SHAMPOO IS NEEDED TO CLEAN YOUR HAIR.

❈ USE FINGERTIPS NOT FINGERNAILS TO CREATE A LATHER AND MASSAGE YOUR SCALP.

❈ RINSE HAIR THOROUGHLY AND COMPLETELY BETWEEN WASHINGS.

❈ TO REMOVE SHAMPOO RESIDUE TRY VINEGAR RINSE ON PAGE 23.

❈ WASH WITH WARM WATER AND RINSE WITH COOL WATER FOR SHINY HAIR.

❈ APPLY YOUR FAVORITE CONDITIONER TO YOUR HAIR. WRAP YOUR HEAD WITH A FLUFFY TOWEL. LIE BACK IN THE TUB AND RELAX FOR 10 MINUTES.

❈ PAT HAIR DRY. DON'T SCRUB.

❈ COMB HAIR STARTING AT ENDS. USE A BROAD TOOTH COMB TO HELP PREVENT BREAKAGE.

"Genius is of small use to a woman who does not know how to do her hair." EDITH WHARTON

"SOME YOUNG AND SAUCY DANDELIONS STOOD LAUGHING IN THE SUN; THEY WERE BRIMMING FULL OF HAPPINESS, AND RUNNING O'ER WITH FUN..." ANONYMOUS ♥ THE DANDELION FLOWER MEANS "FAITHFULNESS" & "ORACLE" ♥ ROMANTIC IDEA: SHAMPOO YOUR HUBBY ♥ DANDELION ♥

Mayonnaise Hair Pack

* YOU WILL PROBABLY WANT TO CUT THE RECIPE IN HALF IF YOU HAVE SHORT HAIR. THIS TREATMENT MAY RELAX A PERM.

So many worlds,
So much to do,
So little done,
Such things to be.

TENNYSON

MAYO

Salad for your hair! Very rich and moisturizing...*
Mix ¼ cup real mayonnaise & ⅓ cup smashed avocado. Work through clean hair. Wrap hair in a towel. Leave on for ½ hour. Rinse. Wash with your favorite shampoo.

30

"Since once I sat upon a promontory, and heard a mermaid on a dolphin's back uttering such dulcet and harmonious breath, that the rude sea grew civil at her song, and certain stars shot madly from their spheres to hear the sea-maid's music."

William Shakespeare

Stress-Relieving Massage & Aromatherapy

On being asked what she wore to bed: "Chanel No. 5."
— Marilyn Monroe

"Take the gentle path." George Herbert
Transforming Self Massage

"I have said that poetry is the spontaneous overflow of

one: Sit up straight, and shrug your shoulders toward your ears. Hold for six seconds. Release. Repeat.

two: Roll your shoulders in a circular motion. First forward, then backward. Slowly rotate head clockwise, & then counterclockwise.

three: Gently squeeze the back of your neck with your right hand. Massage from the top of the neck all the way down to the shoulder. Repeat with the left hand on the other side.

four: Gently press the base of your skull with your thumb. Hold for 5 seconds. Repeat on tense spots all the way down to the top of the spine.

"in tranquility." -Wordsworth emotion recollected

powerful feelings: it takes its origin from

Classic Almond Massage Oil

In a dark glass bottle, combine: 2/3 cup wheat germ oil, 1/3 cup grape seed oil, 15 drops vitamin E oil, & 10 drops almond-scented perfume oil. Shake well. Use for massage or as a moisturizer. Great as an addition to a honeymoon gift basket!

8 oz.

"The first wealth is health." Emerson

SPA MASSAGE

A simple spa massage. Enjoy this massage with someone special to you. Before you begin you'll need:

A firm mattress or massage table
A pillow
A fitted sheet & beach towel
Almond massage oil
Spa music
A warm, dimly lit room

1.) Wash hands and trim finger nails. 2.) Have person receiving massage lie on their back. Cover him/her with a beach towel. 3.) Apply oil to your hands. 4.) Massage throat gently, rubbing side to side. 5.) Massage face using soft upward strokes. Start at the chin move toward the forehead. Using finger tips, massage along sides of nose and across bridge of nose. Use circu-

"Where there is great love there are always miracles."

35

lar strokes to massage forehead and cheeks. 6.) Massage crown of head with finger tips. Move to the back and sides of head. 7.) Massage muscles in arms. Start with the hands and move all the way up to the shoulders. 8.) Firmly massage muscles in each leg. Start with feet and move up to hips. 9.) Have the person turn over. 10.) Apply oil to the back and gently stroke with the palms of your hands. 11.) Using thumbs, massage shoulders, neck, upper back, between shoulder blades, along spine, and lower back. 12.) Knead all of the back muscles firmly and deeply.

"Live each season as it passes; breathe air, drink the drink, taste the fruit, and resign yourself to the influences of each. Let them be your only diet drink and botanical medicines."

HENRY DAVID THOREAU

Wisdom from the Pen of Willa Cather...

SCALP MASSAGE

"We do not remember days, We remember moments."
Cesare Pavese ~

THIS TREATMENT STIMULATES THE CIRCULATION IN YOUR SCALP, AND HAIR GROWTH.

Rinse your hair with warm water. Massage your entire scalp using your fingertips. Add 1 tablespoon olive oil to your hair and massage for 2 minutes using a circular motion. Wrap your hair in a towel, or cover it with a plastic shower cap. Sit back and relax for 20 minutes. Shampoo hair and rinse well.

For a scalp massage that doubles as a relaxing aromatherapy treatment, add a couple drops of your favorite essential oil to the olive oil before adding it to your hair. (One of my favorites is Love oil by AVEDA. ♥)

Reflexology

Reflexologists believe that applying pressure to specific reflex points in the feet will benefit corresponding parts of the body. They also believe that reflexology improves circulation, relieves stress, and calms your mind & spirit. Apply pressure to all the reflex points in both feet for a well rounded massage experience.

BIRKENSTOCK SANDALS- TRENDY AND OH SO COMFORTABLE!

"Life was meant to be lived and curiosity must be kept alive. One must never, for whatever reason, turn his back on life." Eleanor Roosevelt

massage each reflex point and feel good from head to toe!

sinuses
neck
head
eye
ear
Shoulder
stomach
lung
heart
kidney
liver
Spinal column
colon
hip
knee
bladder
Sciatic Nerve

❤ essential oils & their qualities ❤

i n Shakespeare's _Hamlet_, Ophelia describes a bouquet of flowers and gives each one a meaning. Herbs have meanings too. When using the following essential oils in your spa recipes, ponder the meaning behind each herb.

basil: (Basileus) means "king". Said to have grown at the sight of the crucifixion. Calms nerves. Stimulates memory. Clove like aroma.

Camomile: (Chamaemelum Nobile) means "energy in adversity." Induces sleep. Soothes, relaxes and refreshes.

Cedarwood: (Cedrus) means "strength". Relaxes. Sensual scent.

Clary sage: (Salvia sclarea) means "domestic virtue." Refreshing. Sometimes used to flavor wine.

eucalyptus: (Eucalyptus) means "to cover." Clears nasal passages. Soothes. Cools. Invigorates.

frankincense: (Boswellia) means "free & pure." Calming.

geranium : (Geranium) means "comforting." Relaxing. Soothing.

ginger : (Zingiber Officinale) means "lively." Calming. Sharpens the senses.

jasmine : (Jasminum) Also called Jessamine. Means "amiability." Grown in France and Morocco. Soothing and fragrant.

lavender : (Lavendula) means "distrust." A favorite, classic, old-world plant. Healing. Energizing.

lemongrass : (Cymbopogon Citratus) means "cheer." Rejuvenating.

myrrh : (Commiphora) means "gladness." Relieves stress.

neroli : Distilled from orange blossoms. Named for 17th princess of Nerola, Anna Maria. Orange blossoms mean "purity." Uplifting.

patchouli : (Pogostemon Cablin) means "virtue." Also called love oil. Soothing.

Note: Never use essential oils undiluted. Store in dark glass bottles.

light as feathers, smelling sweet : and it would

garden mist potpourri

...And how well I remember the sweet, subdued scent of pot-pourri, for as well as flowers there were in every room big open bowls of the pot-pourri she loved to have about her. ~ E.S. Rhode ♥

Ingredients:
- 1 oz Lemon Verbena
- 1 oz Orange Blossom
- 1 oz Lavender
- 1 oz Rose
- 2 oz Rosemary
- 1 oz Lemon Thyme
- 1 oz Peppermint
- 1 oz Sage
- 2 tbs. Crushed Cardamom
- 2 tbs. Crushed Cinnamon Sticks
- 1 oz Crushed, Dried Orange Peel
- 3 tbs. Orris Root Powder
- 2 drops Lavender Oil
- 2 drops Lemon Oil
- 2 drops Neroli Oil

♥

To Create Pot-Pourri:
Thoroughly dry all of the flowers and herbs. In a large bowl, mix flowers, herbs, spices, citrus peel & orris root powder. Add the oils one drop at a time. Combine well after each drop. Seal pot-pourri tightly into zip-lock bags for 2 months to properly age. Shake bag every other day to blend evenly. ♥

Ideas:
- Display in a large pot-pourri bowl on coffee table.
- Give pot-pourri as a gift.
- Put it in a pretty jar or sew some into a sachet for a drawer or closet.
- Simmer in a pot-pourri pot for the ultimate spa experience! ♥

strew (strŌŌ) *tr. v.* strewed, strewn
(strŌŌn) or strewing, strews. 1. To
spread about; scatter. 2. To cover
(an area) with things scattered
or sprinkled.

Treading on dreams...

A luxury of old... Nebuchadnezzar of Persia indulged
by strewing rosepetals in the many rooms of his palace.
The Romans dined in halls adorned with flower petals.
Royalty enjoyed showers of flowers & herbs at corona-
tions and other special occasions. Some blooms &
herbs for your strewing pleasure: roses, daisies, fennel,
lavender, marjoram, penny royal, mint, sage, tansey, violets, savory, germander, lemon balm, bay, juniper, lilac,
apple blossom & myrtle.

A longing fulfilled is sweet to the soul. Proverbs 13:9

Aromatherapy in Every Room

Vanilla Room Spray – Add 6 to 10 drops pure, white vanilla extract to 12 oz. water in a spray bottle. Use as a room or linen spray.

Open the windows after it rains.

Drink China Rosepetal tea (by Taylors of Harrogate) from your favorite cup.

Plant floral topiaries & make scented tussie mussies!

Create garlands from dried apple & orange slices, cinnamon sticks, and eucalyptus sprigs.

Fresh flowers... mmm! Plant a window herb garden in little pots & china teacups or creamers.

Hang a bunch of eucalyptus in your shower.

Refresh Stick-Ups by spraying the tired scent disc with your favorite scent.

Add 3 drops lemon oil to the water in your iron for scented steam.

Add 4 or 5 drops essential oil to a small box of baking soda. Sprinkle on carpet before vacuuming.

Bake cinnamon swirl bread.

43

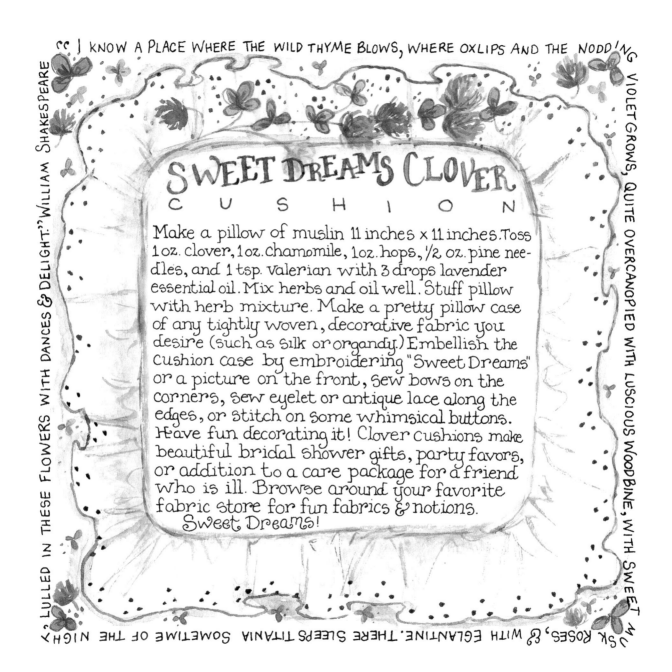

SWEET DREAMS CLOVER
C U S H I O N

Make a pillow of muslin 11 inches x 11 inches. Toss 1 oz. clover, 1 oz. chamomile, 1 oz. hops, ½ oz. pine needles, and 1 tsp. valerian with 3 drops lavender essential oil. Mix herbs and oil well. Stuff pillow with herb mixture. Make a pretty pillow case of any tightly woven, decorative fabric you desire (such as silk or organdy.) Embellish the cushion case by embroidering "Sweet Dreams" or a picture on the front, sew bows on the corners, sew eyelet or antique lace along the edges, or stitch on some whimsical buttons. Have fun decorating it! Clover cushions make beautiful bridal shower gifts, party favors, or addition to a care package for a friend who is ill. Browse around your favorite fabric store for fun fabrics & notions.
Sweet Dreams!

Celestial Shell Candles

Honeysuckle scented candles! Warm candlelight is a soothing and romantic element of your Spa experience. To make these you'll need:

12 oz. natural beeswax   1 pinch ground cinnamon

12 oz. paraffin wax   8 drops honeysuckle candle perfume

½ oz. dried honeysuckle flowers   2½ oz. stearin

Wash large scallop shells well. Dry completely. Melt waxes in a double boiler over low heat (15-20 minutes) Melt the stearin. Add dried flowers and stearin to wax. Sprinkle in cinnamon. Mix completely. Cut candle wicking to about 2½ inches. Attach to a metal wick holder. Pour the hot wax into shells one at a time. Place wicks, attached to holders, in shells. Allow candles to cool, undisturbed, for one hour.

"Outside the open window... the morning air is all awash with angels..."
RICHARD PURDY WILBUR

~BROWNING~
How do I love thee?
Let me count the
ways? I love thee
to the depth and
breadth and height
my soul can
reach being

SCENTED INK

SEALED WITH A KISS • KISS • A KISS • SEAL • KISS • A KISS • KISS • SEALED WITH A KISS • SEALED WITH A KISS • SEALED WITH A KISS • SEALED WITH A KISS • SEALED WITH A KISS • A KISS • SEALED

Here's a fun way to write love letters, or just keep in touch. As soon as that special someone opens the envelope they'll be delighted by the rich scent of lemon verbena.

Crumble 2 oz. dried lemon verbena into a small saucepan. Add 1 cup water. Bring to a boil. Lower heat and simmer the mixture down to 4 tablespoons brown liquid. Strain well. Mix liquid with 2½ oz. India ink. Using a small funnel, pour ink into a decorative, glass, ink bottle.

"Sir, more than kisses, letters mingle souls; For, thus friends absent speak."
– John Donne

Me ♥
Honey Bunny
Lovers Lane
MN

SWAK

SEALED

46

God gave all men all earth to love...

but since our hearts are small,

♥

Ordained for each one spot should prove
beloved over all.

'RUDYARD KIPLING

a wagon wheel herb garden

Seeds

Use an actual wagon wheel, or stones & pebbles to mark the "spokes" & "hub" of wheel.

Add compost to your soil to encourage the early growth of herbs in Springtime.

Draw a plan of your herb garden or use the diagram above. (Use your favorites! ☺) Gather your gardening tools and seeds and head to your garden spot... make it a sunny one! Space seeds according to package directions. Water seeds right after planting to even out soil. Water according to directions thereafter. Harvest on sunny mornings after dew is gone. Hang stems in bunches to dry. Harvest seed heads when brown. Store dried herbs & seeds in airtight containers.

Wheel labels: thyme (p), parsley (b), savory (a), rosemary (p), oregano (p), basil (a), parsley (p), sage (p)

Movies For Friends

Beaches - Bette Midler & Barbara Hershey
Steel Magnolias - Julia Roberts & Sally Field
When Harry Met Sally - Meg Ryan & Billy Crystal
Love Affair - Warren Beatty & Annette Bening
It Could Happen to You - Nicolas Cage & Bridget Fonda
Little Women - Winona Ryder & Susan Sarandon
Made In Heaven - Kelly McGillis & Timothy Hutton
Chances Are - Mary Stuart Masterson & Cybill Shepherd
Fried Green Tomatoes - Kathy Bates & Jessica Tandy
Sabrina - Harrison Ford & Julia Ormond
Circle of Friends - Minnie Driver & Chris O'Donnell
Anne of Green Gables - Megan Follows & Colleen Dewhurst
Anne of Avonlea - Megan Follows & Colleen Dewhurst
Working Girl - Harrison Ford & Melanie Griffith
The Mirror Has Two Faces - Barbra Streisand
9 to 5 - Dolly Parton & Jane Fonda
Don't Tell Her It's Me - Steve Guttenberg & Jami Gertz
French Kiss - Meg Ryan & Kevin Kline
You've Got Mail - Meg Ryan & Tom Hanks

"The endearing elegance of female friendship"

POPCORN

JOHNSON

Luxurious
Pampering
For
Hands
&
Feet

51

♥ Soft ♥ hands ♥ treatment ♥

You _can_ have beautiful hands overnight! This treatment is especially good in the winter months when skin gets chapped and dry.

1.) Wash hands with a moisturizing soap or mild facial cleanser. Rinse & pat dry.

2.) Rub moisturizing lotion on hands. Pay close attention to the skin around cuticles and knuckles.

3.) Carefully pull on each finger to stretch. Apply pressure to the palm of each hand (one at a time.)

4.) Generously apply petroleum jelly to both hands and cover with gloves overnight.

5.) In the morning, remove gloves. Wash and rinse hands completely.

♥ five ♥ minute ♥ manicure ♥

Remove nail polish from nails. Push cuticles back with an orange wood stick. File rough nail edges. (Only file nails in one direction!) Apply a clear base coat. Apply two coats of your favorite colored nail polish. Seal with a protective clear top-coat. Make sure you allow sufficient drying time between coats. Plunge both hands into a large bowl of ice water to quick-dry.

tip: for healthy cuticles and finger nails, rub vitamin E oil on them daily. Vitamin E oil will also protect nails from chlorine, so be sure to apply plenty before swimming.

"'Adieu!' she cries; and waved her lily hand."
JOHN GAY

52

Elder Flower Cream
for pretty, soft hands ♥

"**N**ow join your hands, and with your hands your hearts." ♥ William Shakespeare...

Place 6 oz. petroleum jelly and ½ oz. beeswax in a glass baking dish. Melt over low heat (but don't boil). Stir in 3 oz. fresh elder flowers & 1 oz. fresh marigold petals. Cover baking dish. Place in a 200°F oven for 4 hours. Strain into a decorative pot. Allow cream to cool completely before covering.

"Man may work from sun to sun, But woman's work is never done." anonymous

- Melt cubes of paraffin in a double boiler.
- Allow to cool slightly.
- Dip hands into wax while still warm. Wait 5 minutes. Peel off.

"To love oneself is the beginning of a life-long romance." OSCAR WILDE

Enclosed:
Recipe for
Paraffin Paradise
Hand Beautifier

"The Royal Treatment" Princess Pedicure

Remove old nail polish from toes. Trim toenails and smooth edges with an emery board or file. Soak feet in a basin filled with warm water + 1 cup of scented bath salts. If bottoms of feet are rough or calloused, rub them smooth with a pumice stone. Clean feet with a foot brush and soap. Dry feet with a towel. Apply a heavy moisturizing cream on feet and legs. (My favorite is Sween Cream :) Using circular strokes, massage cream into skin. Tug gently on each toe. Massage arch, heel, and top of each foot. Massage the base of each toe. Elevate feet for 20 minutes & read your favorite magazine. Finish pedicure by pushing back cuticles with an orangewood stick. Apply 2 coats nail polish.

• NOTE: Women who are pregnant, diabetics, and people with circulation problems should avoid doing this and other foot & leg treatments.

"I will make you brooches & toys for your delight. Of bird-song at morning & star-shine at night. I will make a palace fit for you and & me. Of green days in forests and blue days at sea. I will make my kitchen and you shall keep your room where white flows the river and bright blows the broom, and you shall wash your linen in rainfall at morning..."

"...& dewfall at night"
R. L. STEVENSON

Peppermint Pinwheel

FOOT LOTION

Great for foot massages! Mix the following ingredients together and indulge in the paradise of peppermint pinwheels!

1 teaspoon pure aloe vera gel
3 Tablespoons unscented lotion
5 drops peppermint oil

Yield: 1 treatment

3 Seaside Beauty Treatments

"As idle as a painted ship upon a painted ocean." – Samuel Taylor Coleridge

beach foam foot bath (1 Treatment)

EASE SORE FEET AND MELT AWAY STRESS. COMBINE EPSOM SALT OR BATH CRYSTALS WITH YOUR FAVORITE PERFUME OIL. POUR SALT MIXTURE INTO A BIG BASIN OF WARM WATER. SOAK FEET FOR 20 MINUTES. RUB ROUGH HEELS AND SOLES WITH A PUMICE STONE. YOU CAN STOP HERE OR CONTINUE ON WITH THE "PRINCESS PEDICURE" OR TRY THE "PARAFFIN PARADISE HAND TREATMENT" ON YOUR FEET.

"...She passed the salley gardens with little snow-white feet..." – YEATS

sandbar footsie treatment (1 Treatment)

AN EXFOLIATING, SMOOTHING TREATMENT FOR FEET. MIX 1/2 CUP SAND, 1 TABLESPOON SEA SALT, AND 1/2 CUP OLIVE OIL IN A BOWL. MASSAGE FEET WITH THE SAND MIXTURE OVER A BIG BASIN. RINSE FEET IN A BASIN OF COOL WATER. PAT FEET DRY WITH A TOWEL.

"The anchor heaves, the ship swings free, The sails swell full. To sea, to sea!"

– THOMAS LOVELL BEDDOES

CABANA sea weed wrap (1 Treatment)

STIMULATE CIRCULATION & MOISTURIZE DRY SKIN! IN A BIG BOWL, COMBINE 2 CUPS CLAY, 1 CUP KELP POWDER, 3/4 CUP LEMON JUICE AND 4 DROPS SANDALWOOD OIL. TAKE A QUICK SHOWER AND SCRUB DOWN WITH A LOOFAH. STAND IN BATHTUB AND RUB SEAWEED (KELP) MIXTURE ALL OVER YOUR BODY, STARTING WITH YOUR FEET. WRAP GAUZE SNUGLY AROUND SEAWEED MIXTURE. WRAP TOES FIRST AND WRAP ALL THE WAY TO THE TOP OF EACH LEG. REPEAT ON ARMS, TORSO, AND HAIR (BUT NOT YOUR FACE ☺) LAY IN YOUR TUB AND COVER UP WITH FLUFFY TOWELS. AFTER 1/2 HOUR, UN-WRAP GAUZE. SHOWER WITH LUKE WARM WATER. PAT DRY. WASH GAUZE STRIPS AND USE AGAIN. "A man may stand there [Cape Cod] and put all America behind him."

– HENRY DAVID THOREAU (CAPE COD 1865)

"The sea is the land's edge also... earlier and other creation: The starfish, the hermit crab, the whale's backbone; The pools where it offers to our curiosity. The more delicate algae and the sea anemone. It tosses up our losses, the torn seine; The shattered lobster pot, the broken oar. And the gear of foreign dead men. The sea has many voices." Thomas Stearns Eliot.

There is pleasure in the pathless woods,
There is a rapture in the lonely shore,
There is society, where none intrudes,
By the deep sea and the music in its roar :
I love not man the less, but nature more.
                    Lord Byron ~

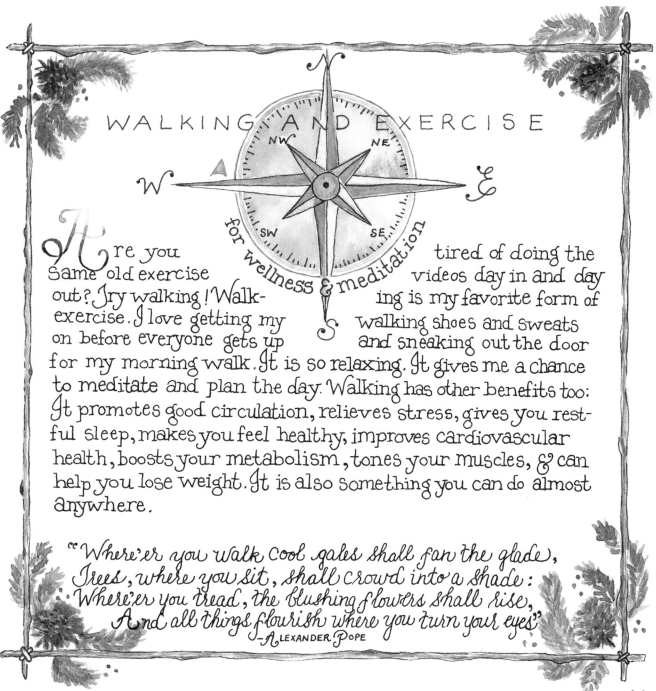

WALKING AND EXERCISE

for wellness & meditation

Are you tired of doing the same old exercise videos day in and day out? Try walking! Walking is my favorite form of exercise. I love getting my walking shoes and sweats on before everyone gets up and sneaking out the door for my morning walk. It is so relaxing. It gives me a chance to meditate and plan the day. Walking has other benefits too: It promotes good circulation, relieves stress, gives you restful sleep, makes you feel healthy, improves cardiovascular health, boosts your metabolism, tones your muscles, & can help you lose weight. It is also something you can do almost anywhere.

"Where'er you walk cool gales shall fan the glade,
Trees, where you sit, shall crowd into a shade:
Where'er you tread, the blushing flowers shall rise,
And all things flourish where you turn your eyes."
—Alexander Pope

60

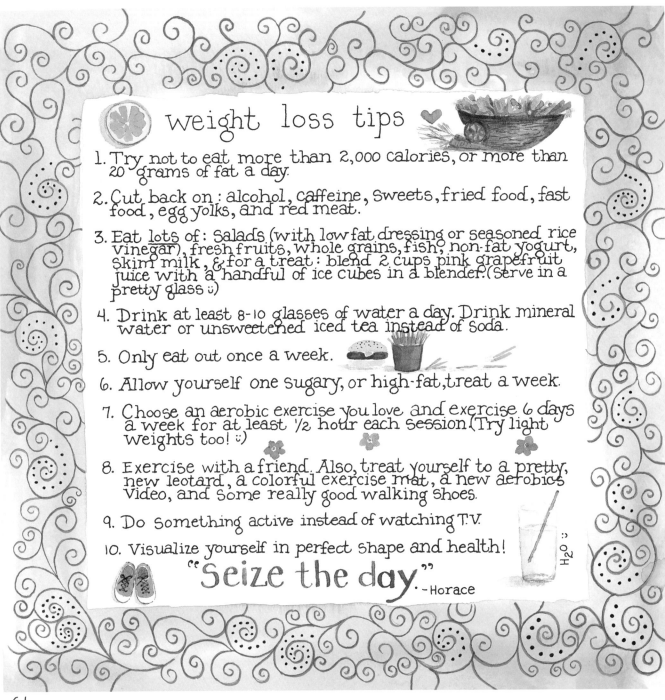

weight loss tips

1. Try not to eat more than 2,000 calories, or more than 20 grams of fat a day.

2. Cut back on: alcohol, caffeine, sweets, fried food, fast food, egg yolks, and red meat.

3. Eat lots of: salads (with low fat dressing or seasoned rice vinegar), fresh fruits, whole grains, fish, non-fat yogurt, skim milk, & for a treat: blend 2 cups pink grapefruit juice with a handful of ice cubes in a blender. (Serve in a pretty glass ☺)

4. Drink at least 8-10 glasses of water a day. Drink mineral water or unsweetened iced tea instead of soda.

5. Only eat out once a week.

6. Allow yourself one sugary, or high-fat, treat a week.

7. Choose an aerobic exercise you love and exercise 6 days a week for at least ½ hour each session. (Try light weights too! ☺)

8. Exercise with a friend. Also, treat yourself to a pretty, new leotard, a colorful exercise mat, a new aerobics video, and some really good walking shoes.

9. Do something active instead of watching T.V.

10. Visualize yourself in perfect shape and health!

"Seize the day." —Horace

H₂O ☺

Spa Foods and Cooking Light

"Thank you for calling the Weight Loss Hotline. If you'd like to lose ½ pound right now, press 1 eighteen thousand times."

~ GLASBERGEN

"Breakfast in bed is paradise found!" M. Placzek

BREAKFAST ♥ PARFAIT ♥

This tempting, creamy, dessert-like breakfast will satisfy your hunger and your sweet tooth!

Simply layer yogurt, granola (or your yogurt & Enjoy in the dessert, or as a cherry-vanilla and blueberries favorite flavor fresh fruit.) morning, as a snack... Yummy!

"LIFE, WITHIN DOORS, HAS FEW PLEASANTER PROSPECTS THAN A NEATLY ARRANGED AND WELL-PROVISIONED BREAKFAST TABLE." *Nathaniel Hawthorne*

"ALL THEY COULD SEE WAS SKY, WATER, BIRDS, LIGHT, AND CONFLUENCE. IT WAS THE WHOLE MORNING WORLD." *Eudora Welty*

Breakfast is Served...

"SIGHT READ HIS STORY Walden...

"POVERTY WILL NOT BE POVERTY, NOR WEAKNESS WEAKNESS."

Home ♥ Made
Health Nuts Cereal
SUPER DOOPER YUMMY, CRUNCHY, LIGHT & HEALTHY!

- ♥ 3½ CUPS WHOLE WHEAT FLOUR
- ♥ 1 CUP DARK BROWN SUGAR
- ♥ 1 TEASPOON SALT
- ♥ 1 TEASPOON BAKING SODA
- ♥ 1 TEASPOON GROUND CINNAMON

- ♥ ⅛ TEASPOON GRATED, FRESH NUTMEG
- ♥ ½ TEASPOON UNSWEETENED COCOA POWDER
- ♥ 2 CUPS LOWFAT BUTTERMILK
- ♥ 3 TEASPOONS REAL VANILLA EXTRACT

PREHEAT OVEN TO 350°F.

IN A BIG MIXING BOWL, COMBINE THE FIRST 7 INGREDIENTS. ADD THE BUTTERMILK AND VANILLA. MIX WELL. OIL A FLAT 12x16 INCH BAKING PAN & SPREAD MIXTURE ONTO IT EVENLY. BAKE FOR ABOUT 25 MINUTES 'TIL BROWNED. BATTER WILL PULL AWAY FROM EDGES OF PAN. REMOVE FROM PAN. COOL FOR 8 HOURS. PREHEAT OVEN TO 275°F. BREAK BATTER INTO PIECES AND PULSE IN A BLENDER. ONLY PULSE IN SMALL AMOUNTS. CRUMBS SHOULD BE COARSE. DIVIDE CRUMBS AND PLACE ON 2- 12x16 INCH BAKING PANS. BAKE FOR 35 MINUTES, STIRRING EVERY 5 MINUTES. ALLOW TO COOL COMPLETELY. STORE IN AN AIRTIGHT CONTAINER. SERVE WITH MILK & FRESH FRUIT, IN PLACE OF GRANOLA IN A BREAKFAST PARFAIT, OR AS AN ICE CREAM TOPPING! ☺

"Oh, it's nice to get up in the mornin', But it's nicer to lie in bed." SIR HARRY LAUDER ♥

"Go CONFIDENTLY IN THE DIRECTION OF YOUR DREAMS! LIVE THE LIFE YOU'VE IMAGINED! AS YOU SIMPLIFY YOUR LIFE, THE LAWS OF THE UNIVERSE WILL BE SIMPLER, SOLITUDE WILL NOT BE SOLITUDE, POVERTY WILL NOT BE POVERTY...

Peachy·Morning·Muffins·

1 cup all-purpose flour
1 cup whole wheat flour
1 cup brown sugar
2 tsp. baking soda
2 tsp. cinnamon
½ tsp. salt
¼ tsp. ground cloves
⅛ tsp nutmeg
2 cups peeled & cubed peaches
½ cup shredded apples

½ cup shredded coconut
½ cup currants or raisins
1 tsp. grated lemon peel
½ cup chopped pecans (if desired)
¼ cup canola oil
½ cup apple sauce
¼ cup milk
2½ tsp. real vanilla
2 eggs (or just egg whites)

Preheat oven to 350°F. Spray 18 muffin tin cups with cooking spray, or use paper liners (they come in lots of different colors and patterns…I love ones with hearts ☺) In a large mixing bowl, combine all dry ingredients & spices. Add fruits and nuts. Mix well. Add wet ingredients & eggs. Stir just until moistened. Fill muffin tin cups 3/4 full. Bake for 25 minutes, or until toothpick inserted in center of a muffin comes clean. Remove from pan immediately. Serve warm or cool.

"O, do you know the muffin man?"

Hippy Shakes

A tasty power shake to enjoy after working out...

In a bar blender combine the following...
2 cups chocolate frozen yogurt
1/4 cup peanut butter
1/4 cup coconut milk (or more to blend)
1 Tablespoon wheat germ
1 Tablespoon protein powder

Garnish with shredded coconut, carob chips, & granola...

"Those who make peaceful revolution impossible will make violent revolution inevitable." John Fitzgerald Kennedy

Groovy

TROPICAL ISLAND

Refreshing, fruity, creamy, satisfying & light! What more could you ask for? Use a bar blender for these recipes. (2 serv. each)

JAMAICAN MELON MINT: Blend 2¼ c. diced, fresh honeydew melon, 1 kiwi, 2 Tablespoons fresh spearmint, 1 Tablespoon fresh lime juice, ½ c. lemon lime soda & 7 ice cubes.

SECLUDED BEACH: 1¼ c. guava juice, 2 teaspoons fresh lime juice, 2 teaspoons fresh lemon juice, 2¼ c. diced, fresh mango, 1 ripe banana & 1 c. ice.

HAWAIIAN PINA COLADA: 1¼ c. coconut milk, 2 c. vanilla frozen yogurt, 1 c. diced pineapple, 1 fresh banana & 1 Tablespoon orange juice.

TANGERINE TANGO: 1½ c. orange juice, 2 c. fresh tangerine sections, 1 cup diced, fresh papaya, 1 c. orange sherbet & 6 ice cubes.

DESERTED ISLAND PARADISE: 2 c. vanilla frozen yogurt, ¼ c. fresh peaches, ⅓ c. frozen cherries, 1 teaspoon vanilla extract, ¼ c. skim or 2% milk.

"As we looked far seaward among the outer islands, the trees seemed to march seaward still, going steadily over the heights and down to the water's edge."

—Sarah Orne Jewett

67

FRUIT SMOOTHIES

ARUBA CHOCOLATE RASPBERRY: 2c. chocolate frozen yogurt, 1/4 c. fresh or frozen raspberries, 6 oz vanilla yogurt, 1/4 c. milk.

TAHITIAN TROPICAL: 2c. lemon sherbet, 1/2 c. fresh strawberries, 1 kiwi, 1 teaspoon lime juice.

FLORIDA KEYS CREAMSICLE: 2 c. vanilla frozen yogurt, 1 orange, peeled and sectioned, 1/2 - 1 teaspoon vanilla extract, 1/4 c. skim milk.

♥ Ideas for Morning Romance... ♥

- Breakfast in bed while listening to The London Symphony Orchestra and sharing the morning paper.

- Coffee from a thermos, fresh bagels & cream cheese, and feeding the ducks from a park bench.

- Watching a sunrise • tea for two • Outdoor cafes

- farmers markets -- buy flowers, fresh bread & produce ☺

- exercise together and go out to breakfast

- For a special occasion: Arrange to have a champagne breakfast in a hot air balloon.

- Sunday brunch & a Sunday drive • a morning walk & bird-watching

- Breakfast at Tiffany's -- the movie, the song, or the place! ☺

Each cup of tea represents an imaginary voyage – CATHERINE DOUZEL

Aaaahhh, tea! – ME

Luxuriate in the aroma of green tea & peppermint...

green tea & peppermint medley

Teach us to delight in simple things – RUDYARD KIPLING

6 to 8 CUPS~

Boil water and pour a small amount into a tea pot. Whirl water around the inside to warm the pot. Pour water out. Add 2 to 3 teaspoons green tea & 3 teaspoons peppermint tea leaves to the tea pot. Pour boiling water over the tea. Cover and allow to steep for about 4 minutes under a tea cozy. Serve with honey and lemon.

There is a great deal of poetry and fine sentiment in a chest of tea – RALPH WALDO EMERSON

· ROSEWATER · LEMONADE ·

Wow your friends! ¿ Rosewater lemonade is a refreshing, elegant alternative to regular lemonade or fruit punch. Serve it whenever you want to add a special touch to a celebration.

Simply add 2 tablespoons rosewater (the culinary type that can be purchased at gourmet cooking stores) to ½ gallon pink lemonade. Garnish with fresh mint or unsprayed rosepetals.

"Rose is a rose is a rose is a rose" -STEIN

· ANDI'S · FAVORITE · ICED · TEA

My daughter Andrea requests this beverage every year at the first hint of spring.

Just combine equal parts of lemonade and unsweetened iced tea. Garnish with a lemon slice or a whole strawberry.

"I believe the finest vacation would be, to sail away on an ocean of tea!" - M. PLACZEK ♥

TIME FOR AN...

Old-Fashioned Ice Cream Parlor Treat

Soda Fountain Drinks Without a Lot of Fat! ♥ Yay! ☺

Old Tyme Root Beer Float
Fill a frosty mug with your favorite root beer. Put a scoop of lowfat vanilla ice cream or frozen yogurt on top.

Frothy Egg Cream
Pour 2½ tablespoons chocolate syrup into a 10 oz. glass. Pour ¼ cup 2% milk over syrup. Add about 4 oz seltzer water to the glass. Stir until frothy.

Creamsicle Fountain Treat
Fill a frosty mug with orange soda. Put a scoop of lowfat vanilla ice cream or frozen yogurt on top.

Malted Milk Shake
Pour 1 cup 2% milk and 7 tablespoons malted-milk powder into a blender. Process until smooth. Add 1 pint of your favorite flavor lowfat ice cream, 1 scoop at a time, until mixed completely. For a thinner shake add more milk. For a thicker shake add more ice cream.

"The secret to staying young is to live honestly, eat slowly, and lie about your age."

Lucille Ball

Coffee Can Wheat Bread

•PREHEAT OVEN TO 375°. MAKES 2 LOAVES•

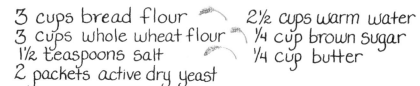

3 cups bread flour
3 cups whole wheat flour
1½ teaspoons salt
2 packets active dry yeast

2½ cups warm water
¼ cup brown sugar
¼ cup butter

In a big mixing bowl, combine 1 cup bread flour, 1 cup whole wheat flour, salt, yeast, and brown sugar. Stir in water. Stir until smooth. Add butter and the rest of the wheat flour. Mix for 5 more minutes. Gradually add enough bread flour to create a stiff dough. Knead for 7 minutes on a lightly floured surface. Place in a buttered bowl, and butter the top of the dough as well. Cover with a clean kitchen towel. Allow to rise until doubled in size (about 1½ hours.) Punch down and knead for 2 minutes to remove air. Divide dough into 2 round loaves. Place in 2 greased 2 lb. coffee cans. Cover and allow to rise for another 40 minutes. Bake at 375° for 45 minutes. Loaves are done when they sound hollow. Remove from cans immediately. Cool on wire racks.

♥ "Brown bread and the Gospel is good fare." MATTHEW HENRY

72

Friendship Salad Buffet ♥

yum!

1.

2.

3.

4.

5.

6.

7.

a celebration of friendship!

You'll need a big nesting bowl and 7 little ones for the various salads that will be served. Make lots of each so the little bowls can be replenished throughout the party. Fill in the spaces around the bowls with fresh carrot and jicama sticks, lemon wedges, edible flowers, pea shoots, fresh parsley and basil, kale, and focaccia wedges. The picture to the left is a numbered diagram for some of the salads you can serve. Don't forget the most important ingredients: good conversation & *friends*.

1. Potato Salad: Make 3 to 6 cups of your favorite potato salad recipe using low fat mayo instead of the fully loaded stuff ☺

2. Apple Slaw: Use the same recipe that is used for the filling of "Stuffed Tomatoes" on next page. (Makes 8+ cups)

3. Cucumber Salad: Mix 1 cup plain, low fat yogurt, 1 tablespoon minced, fresh mint leaves, 1 tablespoon fresh lime juice, and 1 clove finely chopped, fresh garlic. Chill for at least 1 hour. Add 1 very thinly sliced cucumber to chilled dressing. Serve. (Makes about 2 cups)

4. Corn Relish Salad: Mix 1 (16 oz) can whole kernel corn (drained), 1/4 cup water, 1 1/2 cups sweet relish, 1 teaspoon celery seeds, 1 teaspoon mustard seeds and 4 tablespoons diced pimento. Salt & pepper to taste. Chill well before serving. (Makes about 3 cups)

5. Sliced Plum or Cherry Tomatoes: Toss desired amount of sliced plum or cherry tomatoes with your favorite italian salad dressing. Chill. Serve.

6. Greek Salad: Mix 6 cups romaine lettuce, 1/4 cup extra virgin olive oil, 1 large chopped tomato, 2 to 4 tablespoons balsamic vinegar, 24 pitted black olives and 1/2 cup feta cheese chunks. (Makes about 8 cups)

7. Waldorf Salad: Mix 1 cubed red apple, 1 cubed green apple, 2 chopped sticks of celery, 1/2 cup lite mayo, and 1/3 cup chopped walnuts (optional... without the walnuts it's just "Dorf" salad ☺ but, lower in fat.) (Makes about 4 cups)

STUFFED TOMATOES
Served On Cucumber Jelly
(SERVES 8)

Tomato Shells: ABOUT 1/3 OF THE WAY DOWN ON EACH TOMATO, CUT ALL THE WAY AROUND IN ZIG-ZAGS ∧∧∧ TO REMOVE THE TOPS. HOLLOW EACH ONE OUT. SPRINKLE THE INSIDES WITH SALT AND PEPPER. CHILL.

Apple Slaw Stuffing: FINELY SHRED 1 HEAD PURPLE CABBAGE, 1 CARROT, 1 LARGE GREEN ONION, 1 LARGE GREEN APPLE, AND A BIT OF FRESH PARMESAN (2 TSP.) ADD 1 STALK CHOPPED CELERY. IN A SEPARATE BOWL COMBINE 1 TABLESPOON HONEY, 1/2 TEASPOON SALT, 1 TABLESPOON BALSAMIC VINEGAR, AND ENOUGH REAL MAYONNAISE TO MOISTEN. (START WITH 1 TABLESPOON.) COMBINE CABBAGE MIXTURE WITH MAYONNAISE MIXTURE. ADD MORE MAYO IF NEEDED. CHILL 1/2 HOUR. STUFF TOMATOES. TOP WITH SALT, PEPPER, AND A SPRIG OF PARSLEY.

Cucumber Jelly: PEEL AND REMOVE SEEDS FROM 4 LARGE CUCUMBERS. CUT 3 OF THE 4 INTO LITTLE CHUNKS. PURÉE IN BLENDER WITH 1/2 TEASPOON SALT, AND 3 TABLESPOONS FRESH PARSLEY. STRAIN OVER A BOWL FOR ABOUT 1/2 HOUR. THERE SHOULD BE 2 CUPS OF CUCUMBER JUICE. POUR 1 CUP OF THE JUICE INTO TOP PART OF A DOUBLE BOILER THAT HAS SIMMERING WATER IN THE BOTTOM. POUR 2 TEASPOONS UNFLAVORED GELATIN INTO JUICE ON TOP. ALLOW TO DISSOLVE. STIR IN THE RESERVED 1 CUP JUICE, AND 1 TEASPOON TARRAGON VINEGAR. POUR INTO A GLASS BOWL, COVER AND CHILL UNTIL SET (ABOUT 2 HOURS.) BEFORE SERVING, DICE REMAINING CUCUMBER. ADD TO SET JELLY. TO SERVE: SCOOP JELLY EVENLY ONTO SALAD PLATES. PLACE A STUFFED TOMATO IN CENTER OF EACH PLATE.

SKINNY SALAD DRESSINGS

"It's certain that fine women eat a crazy salad with their meat." — Yeats

farmhouse ranch
2 cups

IN A BLENDER, COMBINE: 1½ C. LOWFAT BUTTER-MILK, 4 TABLESPOONS LOWFAT MAYO, 4 TABLESPOONS NONFAT SOUR CREAM, 2 T. FRESH BASIL, 2 T. FRESH CHIVES, 4 TEASPOONS VINEGAR, 2 t. DRY MUSTARD, 2 t. FRESH THYME, 2 GARLIC CLOVES (MINCED), 1 t. SUGAR, SALT & PEPPER TO TASTE. BLEND UNTIL SMOOTH. KEEPS 1 WEEK.

polka dot poppy seed
1 cup

IN A MIXING BOWL, COMBINE: ¼ C. LOWFAT OR NONFAT SOUR CREAM, ¼ C. LOWFAT MAYO, ¼ C. NONFAT, PLAIN YOGURT, ¼ C. FINELY CHOPPED PURPLE ONION, 2 T. POPPY SEED, 2 T. LIME JUICE, 1 T. DIJON MUSTARD, 1 T. HONEY OR CORN SYRUP, ½ t. SALT. MIX WITH A WIRE WHISK, CHILL FOR AT LEAST 1 HOUR BEFORE SERVING. KEEPS 1 WEEK.

lowfat thousand island
2 cups

IN A BLENDER, COMBINE: ⅔ C. LOWFAT MAYO, 4 T. KETCHUP, 4 T. LEMON OR LIME JUICE, 2 T. MINCED GREEN PEPPER, 2 T. MINCED RED BELL PEPPER, 2 T. MINCED GREEN ONION, 2 T. MINCED, FRESH PARSLEY, 2 T. SWEET RELISH, ¼ C WATER, A DASH OF TABASCO, SALT & PEPPER TO TASTE. BLEND UNTIL SMOOTH. KEEPS 1 WEEK.

lite lemon
¾ cup

IN A DRESSING CRUET, COMBINE: ¼ C. OLIVE OIL (EXTRA VIRGIN), ½ t. GRATED LEMON PEEL, ¼ C. LEMON JUICE, ¼ C. WATER, 1 T. DRIED CHIVES, 1 T. PREPARED MUSTARD, 2 T. HONEY, ¼ t. SALT. SHAKE WELL UNTIL MIXED. KEEPS 1 WEEK.

healthy yogurt dill
1½ cups

IN A BLENDER, COMBINE: 1½ C. LOWFAT, PLAIN YOGURT, 1 TABLESPOON LEMON JUICE, AND 3 T. MINCED CUCUMBER, 2-3 t. DILL. BLEND JUST UNTIL MIXED. KEEPS 1 WEEK. (YOU MAY ADD AS MUCH DILL AS YOU LIKE... PICKLE JUICE OR VINEGAR CAN BE SUBSTITUTED FOR THE LEMON JUICE.)

homestyle tomato
1½ cups

IN A MIXING BOWL, COMBINE: ½ C. NONFAT SOUR CREAM, ½ C. V8, 6 T. CHOPPED, FRESH PARSLEY, 4 T. SHERRY VINEGAR OR TARRAGON VINEGAR, 1 T. MINCED, FRESH ONION, 1 t. SALT, ½ t. PEPPER. MIX WELL. KEEPS 1 WEEK.

C = CUP, T = TABLESPOON, t = TEASPOON. ☺

Low fat & Fabulous!

Something DIFFERENT for dinner!

JAPANESE TAKE-OUT

TERIYAKI BOWL

NOODLES

"Don't hang noodles on my ears!" Anonymous

THE FIRST TIME I HAD A TERIYAKI BOWL I WAS VISITING OLD SACRAMENTO, CALIFORNIA. THIS TASTY DISH SEEMS TO BE A COMMON TAKE-OUT ITEM ON MANY OF THE FAST FOOD MENUS OUT THERE. HERE IS MY VERSION OF THIS EASY LITTLE FEAST.

1.) COOK AN 8 OZ. PACKAGE OF CHINESE OR LO MEIN NOODLES ACCORDING TO PACKAGE DIRECTIONS.

2.) STEAM 2 CHOPPED CARROTS, 1 CUP BROCCOLI FLORETS, AND 2½ CUPS SHREDDED CABBAGE UNTIL TENDER.

3.) IN A MEDIUM SAUCEPAN OR SKILLET, COOK 2 LARGE BONELESS, SKINLESS CHICKEN BREASTS (CUT INTO STRIPS) AND 1 - 15 OZ. CAN UNDRAINED STIR FRY MUSHROOMS OVER MEDIUM HEAT. ADD 12 OZ. OF YOUR FAVORITE PREPARED TERIYAKI SAUCE, 2 CHOPPED GREEN ONIONS, AND 1 CLOVE FINELY CHOPPED GARLIC TO THE PAN. HEAT THROUGH UNTIL CHICKEN IS COMPLETELY COOKED.

4.) DIVIDE NOODLES & STEAMED VEGGIES EVENLY BETWEEN 4 PASTA BOWLS. TOP WITH THE TERIYAKI CHICKEN MIXTURE.   (_Serves 4_)

Delicious & Lowfat
SNACK SPREADS

• **Romesco Sauce:** Great as a veggie dip or as a bread spread... Roast almonds by spreading 1/4 cup of them on a cookie sheet and baking at 375° for 10 minutes. Remove them from pan and allow to cool completely. Brown 2 red bell peppers, cut into strips, in a cast iron skillet. Tear pepper strips into pieces and place them in a blender. Add 1/2 cup bread crumbs, 2 pinches cayenne pepper, the almonds, 1 chopped garlic clove, 1/3 cup lowfat salad dressing (Italian or Caesar), and salt & pepper to taste. Purée until desired consistency. Scrape into bowl. Serve at room temp. (Yield: 1 1/4 c.)

• **Yogurt Cream Cheese:** Set a strainer over a mixing bowl (small) and line it with a double layer of cheese cloth. Spoon 1 cup plain yogurt into strainer. Cover and allow to drain in the refrigerator overnight. Will keep in a covered container in fridge, for 4 days. (Yield: 1/2 cup.)

• **Roasted Garlic Purée:** Preheat oven to 400°. Separate garlic head into individual cloves. Keep skin on cloves. Wrap tightly in a piece of aluminum foil. Place in center of oven for 30 minutes, or until garlic cloves are tender. Cool cloves on a plate. Remove skins and mash cloves with a fork. (Yield: 2 tablespoons)

• **Tofu Mayonnaise:** Place 1 cup softened tofu, 2 tablespoons lemon juice or apple cider vinegar, 1/2 teaspoon onion salt, 1 tablespoon prepared mustard, 1 clove minced garlic, and 1 large minced shallot into a blender. Blend until smooth. Add 2 tablespoons vegetable oil. Blend until mixed. (Yield: 1 cup.)

"A WISE MAN ALWAYS EATS WELL." Chinese Proverb

FARMER'S MARKET CORN CHOWDER

Fresh & lots of farmer's market ingredients. Perfect for Company. Serve with a dollop of Sour cream and a hunk of baguette.

Flavorful with

1 teaspoon olive oil (to Sauté)
½ cup chopped purple onion
¼ cup chopped red bell pepper
¼ cup chopped green bell pepper
3 cups fresh corn

3 cups chicken or vegetable broth
⅛ teaspoon cayenne pepper
2-3 potatoes cubed and cooked until tender
2 Tablespoons fresh, chopped parsley.

In a soup pot, Sauté the onion and peppers until onion is transparent. Add remaining ingredients except parsley. Heat through & serve with a bit of parsley as a garnish.

Gladiolus will add the final touch to your dinner table...

♥ farmer's market romance...

Holding hands and sipping coffees, we make our way down a cobblestone street...

Vendors are selling their wares in the early morning mist. Among these simple delicacies... fruits and vegetables, wild honey, ruby red preserves, ropes of garlic, fragrant basil & rosemary, buttery baguettes, and, a myriad of flowers. We select some tomatoes and corn for tonight's dinner... & some gladiolus...

M.P.

MUCH-ADO-ABOUT-CHICKEN-PENNE

the star of the show

Delight in a creamy, savory, and hearty pasta dish with less fat and calories than alfredo.

Marinade:
- ⅓ cup white wine
- 1 teaspoon lime juice
- 1 teaspoon sweet basil
- ½ teaspoon oregano
- ½ teaspoon garlic powder
- ½ teaspoon onion powder
- ¼ teaspoon salt
- pinch of freshly ground pepper

recipe:
- 4 boneless, skinless chicken breasts
- 1 Tablespoon olive oil
- ½ cup chopped onion
- 5 minced garlic cloves
- 2 large portabella mushrooms cut into strips
- ½ teaspoon thyme
- 1 Tablespoon flour
- ⅛ teaspoon nutmeg
- ⅛ teaspoon allspice
- 1 teaspoon celery salt
- pinch of cayenne pepper
- 1-12 oz. can evaporated skim milk
- ½ cup chicken broth
- 12 oz. penne pasta, cooked according to package directions
- 1 Tablespoon chopped, fresh parsley
- paprika

Marinate chicken in combined marinade ingredients for at least 2 hours and up to 8. Preheat oven to 350°. Bake chicken in marinade for 20 minutes, or until juices run clear. Remove chicken from pan and cool. Cut chicken into strips and set juices aside. Sauté onion & garlic in olive oil until tender. Add portabella strips. Cook an additional 4 minutes. Add flour and cook for a few seconds. Add drippings, spices, and milk. Cook until heated through. Add broth and chicken. Heat through. Serve over cooked penne pasta. Garnish with parsley & paprika.

"THERE WAS A STAR DANCED, AND UNDER THAT WAS I BORN."

Entertaining Tip: For a unique party favor idea use tiny picture frames as holders for placecards. Hand-letter each person's name for a more personal touch. (Make sure you buy frames that have little stands :)
Elegant & Thoughtful...

Jill

JAPANESE
garden fare

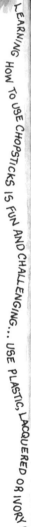

PICTURE A QUIET, SERENE GARDEN IN ANCIENT JAPAN. WEATHERED STONE, MOSSY PATHWAYS, A JIGSAW BRIDGE, BONSAI TREES, LUSH FERNS, AND AN INVITING BAMBOO GARDEN GATE. PASS THROUGH THAT GATE AND STAY AWHILE...

· SHRIMP DUMPLINGS · 24 DUMPLINGS ~

IN A BLENDER, COMBINE 5 OZ. FRESH SHRIMP, SHELLED AND DEVEINED AND 3 OZ. FRESH CRAB LEG MEAT. PULSE UNTIL CHOPPED FINELY AND EVENLY. ADD 1 TABLESPOON SAKE AND 1/8 TEASPOON SALT AND 2 TEASPOONS CORNSTARCH. PULSE UNTIL MIXTURE IS SMOOTH. SPRAY AN OVENPROOF PLATE WITH COOKING SPRAY. DIVIDE THE BLENDED SHRIMP MIXTURE INTO 2 DOZEN EQUAL PORTIONS. FORM EACH PORTION INTO A PATTY. PLACE 8 OF THE DUMPLINGS ON THE PLATE. (YOU WILL BE COOKING THE DUMPLINGS IN 3 SEPARATE BATCHES.) SPRINKLE EACH DUMPLING WITH A BIT OF GROUND GINGER OR, IN THE CENTER OF EACH DUMPLING, PLACE A DAB OF MINCED, PICKLED GINGER. SET THE PLATE OF DUMPLINGS IN A PREPARED STEAMER WHERE THE WATER IS SIMMERING STEADILY. STEAM FOR 2 MINUTES. TRANSFER DUMPLINGS TO AN ATTRACTIVE SERVING DISH. GARNISH WITH FRESH CHIVES OR PARSLEY. SERVE WARM WITH DIPPING SAUCE, SWEET & SOUR, HOT MUSTARD, SOY SAUCE, FISH SAUCE, OR COCKTAIL SAUCE.

Serve white rice or Japanese noodles as a side dish...

· SWEET & SOUR JAPANESE CARROT STICKS · 4 CUPS ~

GATHER THE INGREDIENTS FIRST... THEN PREPARE THE CARROTS... YOU WILL NEED: 1 CUP SEASONED OR PLAIN RICE VINEGAR, 1/3 CUP SUGAR, 1/2 TEASPOON SALT AND 1 POUND OF CARROTS JULIENNED. IN A SAUCEPAN MIX VINEGAR, SUGAR AND SALT OVER MEDIUM HIGH HEAT. STIR UNTIL SUGAR IS DISSOLVED AND MIXTURE IS HEATED THROUGH. PLACE CARROTS IN A HEATPROOF CASSEROLE DISH. POUR SUGAR MIXTURE OVER THEM. ALLOW CARROTS TO "PICKLE" FOR AT LEAST 8 HOURS, COVERED. SERVE CHILLED.

The key to Japanese cuisine: simple, elegant and tasteful... ❀

LEARNING HOW TO USE CHOPSTICKS IS FUN AND CHALLENGING... USE PLASTIC, LACQUERED OR IVORY CHOPSTICKS WHEN DINING & BAMBOO CHOPSTICKS FOR COOKING... OTHERWISE KNOWN AS "QUICK LITTLE ONES."

"*Let the dishes be fewer in number, but exquisitely chosen.*"
~ BRILLAT SAVARIN

· JAPANESE GREEN TEA ICE MILK · SERVES 8-10 ~

MIX 1½ OZ. GREEN TEA POWDER (AVAILABLE AT ORIENTAL MARKETS), AND ½ CUP COGNAC IN A SMALL MIXING BOWL. IN A SEPARATE, LARGER MIXING BOWL, COMBINE 5½ CUPS MILK, ½ CUP CREAM, 1⅓ CUPS NONFAT, INSTANT, POWDERED MILK AND 1¾ CUPS SUGAR. MIX WELL. BOIL MILK MIXTURE IN A LARGE SAUCEPAN OVER MODERATE HEAT. WHEN MILK MIXTURE REACHES A BOIL, REMOVE PAN FROM HEAT AND ALLOW TO COOL UNTIL LUKEWARM. ADD GREEN TEA MIXTURE. COMBINE WELL. FREEZE IN FREEZER UNTIL ICE CRYSTALS FORM AROUND EDGES. PULSE IN A BLENDER JUST LONG ENOUGH TO BREAK UP ICE CRYSTALS. RETURN ICE MILK TO FREEZER. SERVE WHEN ICE MILK IS COMPLETELY SET.

" It was at the highest point in the arc of a bridge that I became aware suddenly of the depth and bitterness of my feelings about modern life, and of the profoundness of my yearning for a more vivid, simple, and peaceable world." JOHN CHEEVER ~

adorn your garden with a handsome stone lantern...

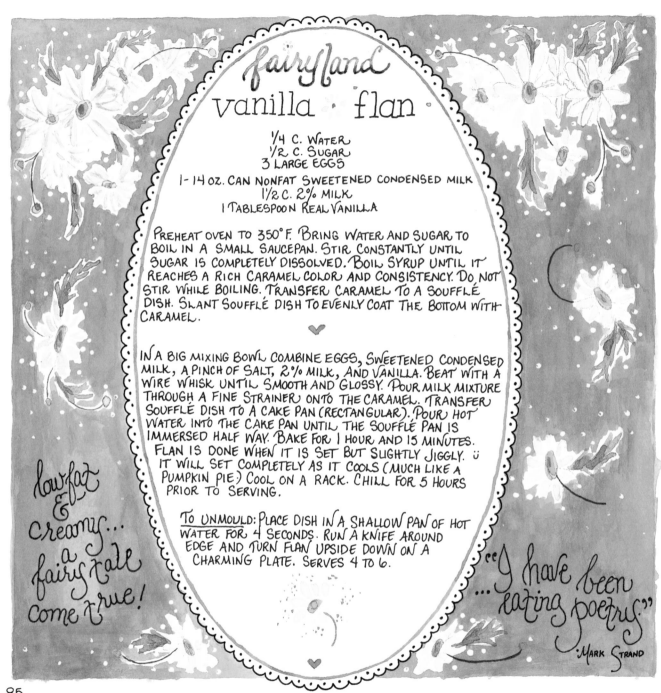

fairyland
vanilla · flan ·

1/4 C. WATER
1/2 C. SUGAR
3 LARGE EGGS
1 - 14 OZ. CAN NONFAT SWEETENED CONDENSED MILK
1 1/2 C. 2% MILK
1 TABLESPOON REAL VANILLA

PREHEAT OVEN TO 350°F. BRING WATER AND SUGAR TO BOIL IN A SMALL SAUCEPAN. STIR CONSTANTLY UNTIL SUGAR IS COMPLETELY DISSOLVED. BOIL SYRUP UNTIL IT REACHES A RICH CARAMEL COLOR AND CONSISTENCY. DO NOT STIR WHILE BOILING. TRANSFER CARAMEL TO A SOUFFLÉ DISH. SLANT SOUFFLÉ DISH TO EVENLY COAT THE BOTTOM WITH CARAMEL.

IN A BIG MIXING BOWL COMBINE EGGS, SWEETENED CONDENSED MILK, A PINCH OF SALT, 2% MILK, AND VANILLA. BEAT WITH A WIRE WHISK UNTIL SMOOTH AND GLOSSY. POUR MILK MIXTURE THROUGH A FINE STRAINER ONTO THE CARAMEL. TRANSFER SOUFFLÉ DISH TO A CAKE PAN (RECTANGULAR). POUR HOT WATER INTO THE CAKE PAN UNTIL THE SOUFFLÉ PAN IS IMMERSED HALF WAY. BAKE FOR 1 HOUR AND 15 MINUTES. FLAN IS DONE WHEN IT IS SET BUT SLIGHTLY JIGGLY. ü IT WILL SET COMPLETELY AS IT COOLS (MUCH LIKE A PUMPKIN PIE.) COOL ON A RACK. CHILL FOR 5 HOURS PRIOR TO SERVING.

TO UNMOULD: PLACE DISH IN A SHALLOW PAN OF HOT WATER FOR 4 SECONDS. RUN A KNIFE AROUND EDGE AND TURN FLAN UPSIDE DOWN ON A CHARMING PLATE. SERVES 4 TO 6.

low fat & creamy... a fairy tale come true!

"...I have been eating poetry."
– MARK STRAND

85

EVERYTHING NICE
Chocolate Chip Cookies

ONLY 3 GRAMS OF FAT!

- ½ cup Sugar
- ¼ cup packed dark brown sugar
- ¼ cup butter, softened
- 2 teaspoons vanilla
- 1 egg white

- ½ cup all-purpose flour
- ½ cup whole wheat flour
- ½ teaspoon baking soda
- ¼ teaspoon salt
- ½ cup mini chocolate chips

Preheat oven to 375°. Combine sugar, brown sugar, butter, vanilla, and egg white in a big mixing bowl. Mix in flours, baking soda and salt. Gently fold in the chocolate chips. Place dough by generous teaspoonfuls onto ungreased cookie sheets. Bake 7-10 minutes. Allow cookies to cool for 5 minutes. Transfer cookies to wire racks & cool completely. Yield: 2 dozen.

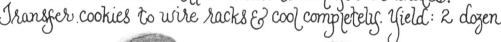

Sugar and Spice and Everything nice...

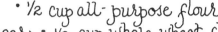

Decadent Vanilla Custard Dip ♥

Combine: One small package instant Vanilla pudding, One cup low-fat milk, and One cup low-fat sour cream in a medium mixing bowl. Serve with a Variety of your favorite fruits & Vanilla Wafers.

Pear

honeydew

Strawberry

Plum

orange

blueberry

Cherry

Mango

Cantaloupe

grape

kiwi

Coconut

apple

banana

raspberry

Pineapple

peach

watermelon

Here are fruits, flowers, leaves and branches,
And here is my heart which beats only for you.

Paul Verlaine

FRENCH PATISSERIE SPA BROWNIES

Chocolate! Need I say more? Enjoy these with a steaming shot of espresso. They're guilt free at only 3 grams of fat apiece!

- 2/3 cup all-purpose flour
- 2/3 cup rolled oats
- 3/4 cup sugar
- 3/4 cup packed brown sugar
- 2/3 cup unsweetened cocoa
- 1/2 teaspoon salt
- 1/2 teaspoon baking powder

- 1/3 cup butter, melted
- 1/3 cup applesauce
- 2 teaspoons real vanilla extract
- 4 eggs slightly beaten
- 1/3 cup mini chocolate chips
- powdered sugar

Heat oven to 350°. Grease and flour a 13 x 9 inch cake pan. In a large bowl, combine first 7 ingredients. Mix well. Add remaining ingredients except the powdered sugar. Stir just to moisten. Pour into prepared pan. Bake at 350° for 25-30 minutes, or until set. Don't overbake! Dust the tops of the brownies with powdered sugar. Cool completely before serving. Yield: 40 brownie squares.

"TEACH US TO DELIGHT IN SIMPLE THINGS."

RUDYARD KIPLING

All
that
is
required
to
feel
that
here
and
now
is
happiness
is
a
simple,
frugal
heart.

• Nikos Kazantzakis 1883-1957 •

More Little Luxuries

"new vistas, new aims..."
~Leigh Hodges

Chin Deep in Bubbles is more than a collection of wonderful recipes and ideas for your bath time. It is a celebration of your creativity and gratitude for life's little luxuries. As you read the last section of my book, I invite you to stretch your imagination and allow these simple rituals to become a part of your life. You will be pleasantly surprised as you begin to notice the little things that make life sweet.

With love from me to you...

Be Well!

Hope ♥ Chests

"THERE IS ALWAYS ONE MOMENT IN CHILDHOOD WHEN THE DOOR OPENS AND LETS THE FUTURE IN." GRAHAM GREENE

EVERY GIRL SHOULD HAVE A HOPE CHEST TO HOUSE HER MEMORIES AND DREAMS FOR THE FUTURE.

IN TIMES OF OLD, IT WAS TRADITIONAL FOR A MOTHER TO GIVE HER DAUGHTER A HOPE CHEST FILLED TO THE BRIM WITH LINENS, LACE, HAND DIPPED CANDLES, HOMEMADE SOAPS, RECIPES AND ALL OF THE OTHER LITTLE THINGS SHE WOULD NEED TO BEGIN KEEPING HOUSE.

WHEN I GRADUATED FROM HIGH SCHOOL AND STARTED COLLEGE MY MOTHER GAVE ME A BEAUTIFUL PINE CHEST WITH LITTLE BLUE AND WHITE FLOWERS AND ROMANTIC GREEN VINES PAINTED ON IT. WHEN I MOVED FROM MY PARENTS HOUSE TO A DORM MY HOPE CHEST HELD THE BRIDE DOLL I INHERITED FROM MY MOM, HAND STITCHED HANDKERCHIEFS, MY PROM DRESS, PICTURES, SCRAPBOOKS AND THE LITTLE PINK HEART MUSIC BOX THAT HUNG ON MY CRIB WHEN I WAS A BABY.

NOW THE CHEST SITS AT THE FOOT OF MY BED. SINCE I MARRIED MY HUSBAND JEFF I'VE ADDED SOME BABY CLOTHES, LINEN SHEETS, KEEPSAKES FROM OUR HONEYMOON, AND VARIOUS NEEDLEWORK PROJECTS. I CONTINUE TO FIND LITTLE THINGS TO ADD TO MY "DREAM" BOX AND I NEVER PLAN ON STOPPING.

Fantasy · Pantry

I AM SO EXCITED! My HUSBAND, DAUGHTER AND I JUST MOVED INTO AN OLD VICTORIAN HOME. I HAVE ALWAYS DREAMED OF OWNING A HOME LIKE THIS, AND IN MY DREAM I INCLUDED A FANTASY PANTRY. THIS UPCOMING SUMMER, I PLAN ON TURNING THIS DREAM INTO A REALITY. WE HAVE A CELLAR TYPE BASEMENT THAT HAS A LITTLE ROOM LINED WITH SHELVES. IT'S A CLEAN, COOL AND DRY SPOT. PERFECT FOR A FANTASY PANTRY! ☺

KEEPING A BEAUTIFUL PANTRY IS A ROMANTIC, CREATIVE WAY TO REKINDLE THE ART OF CANNING AND PUTTING FOOD BY. WHEN ALL OF THE GARDENING, WEEDING, AND HARVESTING ARE DONE YOU CAN PUT ON YOUR PRETTIEST APRON, MAKE SOME OF YOUR BEST SECRET RECIPES, AND ADMIRE THE ROWS OF SPARKLING JARS WITH THEIR JEWEL TONED CONTENTS.

HERE'S WHAT I'M GOING TO DO:
- ♥ PAINT THE WOOD SHELVES HI-GLOSS WHITE AND LINE THEM ALL WITH A PRETTY FLORAL PRINT SHELF PAPER.
- ♥ TACK LACE TO THE EDGES OF THE SHELVES.
- ♥ CUT CIRCLES OF GINGHAM, BURLAP AND CALICO TO PUT ON THE TOPS OF MY JARS (PAPER AND CLOTH DOILIES ARE NICE TOO.) SECURE WITH THIN SILK RIBBON, LACE, STRING, TWINE OR RAFFIA.

♥ BUY THE PRETTIEST CANNING LABELS I CAN FIND AND HAND LETTER EACH JAR APPROPRIATELY.

♥ ARRANGE SHELVES INTO THE FOLLOWING CATEGORIES:
- INFUSED VINEGARS & OILS
- JAMS, JELLIES & PRESERVES
- CHUTNEYS & RELISHES
- HONEYS & SYRUPS
- MUSTARDS & SAUCES
- VEGGIES, FRUITS & PICKLES
- SOUPS
- TEAS, TISANES & POTPOURRIS
- CORDIALS & LIQUEURS

♥ HANG A CURTAIN POLE TO DRY HERBS AND FLOWERS FOR MAKING POTPOURRI AND FOR DRIED FLOWER ARRANGEMENTS. ALSO, HANG GARLIC ROPES AND BUNCHES OF CHILI PEPPERS.

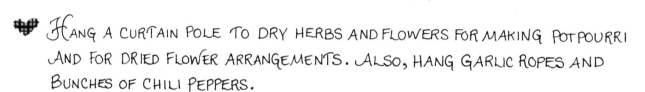

"... he from forth the closet brought a heap of candied apple, quince, and plum, and gourd; with jellies soother than the creamy curd, and lucent syrops, tinct with cinnamon; manna and dates, in argosy transferr'd from Fez; and spiced dainties, every one, from silken Samarcand to cedar'd Lebanon."

John Keats ♥

94

Dreamy Dates For Two ♥

Go to the beach and build a sandcastle. ♥ Have a picnic by a waterfall. ♥ See a comedy show. ♥ Rent a canoe, or rowboat and go fishing. ♥ Go horseback riding. ♥ Plan your dream home together. ♥ Play croquet. ♥ Walk around a lake. ♥ Watch fireworks from a pontoon. ♥ Go to a spa. ♥ Reminisce. ♥ Go backpacking, pick wildflowers, and eat lunch in the woods. ♥ Go on a hot air balloon ride. ♥ Go to a B&B. ♥ Stay in a whirlpool suite. ♥ Take a walk on a beach. ♥ Go to a drive-in movie. ♥ Share an ice cream soda (2 straws! ☺) ♥ Take a train ride. ♥ Enjoy tea for two at a fancy tea room. ♥ Go rollerskating. ♥ Take a trip to Chicago. ♥ Watch a sunset from a porch swing. ♥ Go to an art gallery and have a relaxing lunch at an outdoor cafe afterwards. ♥ Take a gourmet cooking class. ♥ Take an art class. ♥ Bake chocolate chip cookies in your PJs. ♥ Cuddle up on the couch and watch movies. ♥ Have a candlelight dinner in a gazebo. ♥ Read bedtime stories to eachother. (Pick books that you've both always wanted to read and read a little every night.) ♥ Take a bubble bath. ♥ Ride in a horsedrawn carriage in the spring. ♥ Ride in a horsedrawn sleigh with jinglebells in the winter. ♥ Go to a Farmer's Market. ♥ Rent a cabin with a fireplace and a bear rug. ♥ Get dressed up and go to a musical, opera, or play. ♥ Make a memory book. ♥ Enjoy a hammock for two, love poetry and lemonade. ♥ Go antiquing. ♥ Go out for mochas. ♥ Dream. ♥ Go mini golfing. ♥ Go to the zoo. ♥ Go to an amusement park. Take rides on the ferris wheel, merry-go-round and Tilt-a-Whirl. Have corn dogs and cotton candy for supper. ♥ Fly a kite. ♥ Go to a baseball game. ♥ Go to the pet shop and play with the puppies and kittens. ♥ Go sledding or ice skating. ♥ Attend a poetry reading. ♥ Eat truffles and kiss a lot! ♥ Go to the circus. ♥ Visit fairs, carnivals, and festivals. ♥ Watch the clouds. ♥ Gaze at stars. ♥ Go berry picking and make homemade jam. ♥ Go on a hayride in the autumn. ♥ Host a party. ♥ Whisper sweet nothings ♥ Buy "101 Nights of Grrreat Romance" by Laura Corn. ♥ Go to a video arcade. ♥ Go to a jazz bar. ♥ Go to a concert. ♥ Play the romantic board game "Enchanted Evening." ♥ Go Christmas caroling. ♥ Plan and plant a garden. ♥ Make dedication tapes. ♥

95

Good  Deeds

Bring chicken soup to a friend who is ill... mow their lawn... run errands for them. ♥ Pay a teenager's way to summer bible camp ♥ Really listen... be a true friend.   Send a care package to a new mom. Offer to take the baby for a few hours so she can sleep, or have some time to herself. ♥ Give a newly married couple a gift certificate for a meal at a nice restaurant ♥ Play dolls with your daughter or little sister -- play trucks with your son or little brother. Let them know they're worth your time. ♥ Help an elderly neighbor carry in their groceries. Shovel their walk way in winter. ♥ Volunteer to serve food at a homeless shelter. ♥ Greet a new neighbor with a house-warming present or cookies. Invite them over for coffee. ♥ Visit a widow or widower on Memorial day ♥ Visit a nursing home resident on a regular basis. ♥ Be gentle. ♥ Be merciful.♥ Give your spouse a massage or foot rub. ♥ Visit a prisoner and write to them. Tell them about God's love and forgivness. ♥ Spread joy and sunshine.♥ Be generous always! ♥ Be an active member in your church. ♥Admit when you're wrong ♥ Give people compliments-- tell someone how nice they look. ♥ Encourage one another. ♥ Plant a tree ♥ Run a bubble bath for your wife. Remember candles and classical music ♫ ♥Hug your children. ♥ Bring a hot dish to someone who is grieving. Send flowers. ♥ Recycle ♥ Love one another. ♥ Pick up garbage that "litterbugs" left behind ♥ Be a secret Santa to a poor family on Christmas morning. Include a tree, presents, and a turkey for Christmas dinner. ♥ Teach someone a skill you know. ♥ Forgive and make peace. ♥ Be patient. ♥ Bring a bagful of teddy bears to a children's hospital. ♥ Volunteer time to your favorite cause or charity. ♥ Get involved ♥ Put heart shaped sandwiches and love notes in your children's and husband's lunch boxes.♥ Forget a debt owed to you. ♥ Offer to sew layettes for single, expecting mothers. ♥ Give your babysitter and paper boy a bonus for Christmas. ♥ Put garlands of popcorn and cranberries on trees in the winter time! The birds will love you! ♥ Bring your hubby his newspaper and slippers when he gets home from work. Give him some chamomile tea and a shoulder rub to soothe his nerves. ♥ Bring your neighbor flowers from your garden ♥ Always send thankyou notes to show your gratitude. ♥

96

Good Books For Your Quiet Time ♥

Coming Home - Rosamunde Pilcher
Simple Abundance - Sarah Ban Breathnach
Lake Wobegon Days - Garrison Keillor
The Shell Seekers - Rosamunde Pilcher
All Creatures Great and Small - James Herriot
Living a Beautiful Life - Alexandra Stoddard
At Home in Mitford - Jan Karon
Gift From the Sea - Anne Morrow Lindbergh
A Natural History of the Senses - Diane Ackerman
Dandelion Wine - Ray Bradbury
Desiring Italy - Elizabeth Berg
Persian Pickle Club - Sandra Dallas
In and Out of the Garden - Sara Midda
Under the Lilacs - Louisa May Alcott
Too Deep For Tears - Kathryn Lynn Davis
Message In a Bottle - Nicholas Sparks
One Thousand Beautiful Things - Marjorie Barrows
Welcome Home - Emilie Barnes
A Year in Provence - Peter Mayle
The Little Prince - Antoine de Saint-Exupéry
Chocolate For the Woman's Soul - Kay Allenbaugh

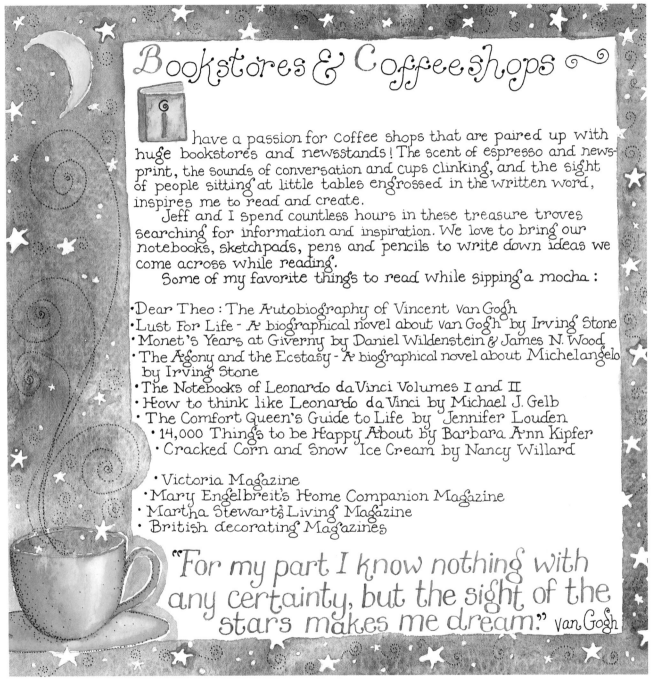

Bookstores & Coffeeshops

I have a passion for coffee shops that are paired up with huge bookstores and newsstands! The scent of espresso and news-print, the sounds of conversation and cups clinking, and the sight of people sitting at little tables engrossed in the written word, inspires me to read and create.

Jeff and I spend countless hours in these treasure troves searching for information and inspiration. We love to bring our notebooks, sketchpads, pens and pencils to write down ideas we come across while reading.

Some of my favorite things to read while sipping a mocha:

- Dear Theo: The Autobiography of Vincent Van Gogh
- Lust For Life - A biographical novel about van Gogh by Irving Stone
- Monet's Years at Giverny by Daniel Wildenstein & James N. Wood
- The Agony and the Ecstasy - A biographical novel about Michelangelo by Irving Stone
- The Notebooks of Leonardo da Vinci Volumes I and II
- How to think like Leonardo da Vinci by Michael J. Gelb
- The Comfort Queen's Guide to Life by Jennifer Louden
- 14,000 Things to be Happy About by Barbara Ann Kipfer
- Cracked Corn and Snow Ice Cream by Nancy Willard

- Victoria Magazine
- Mary Engelbreit's Home Companion Magazine
- Martha Stewart's Living Magazine
- British decorating Magazines

"For my part I know nothing with any certainty, but the sight of the stars makes me dream." van Gogh

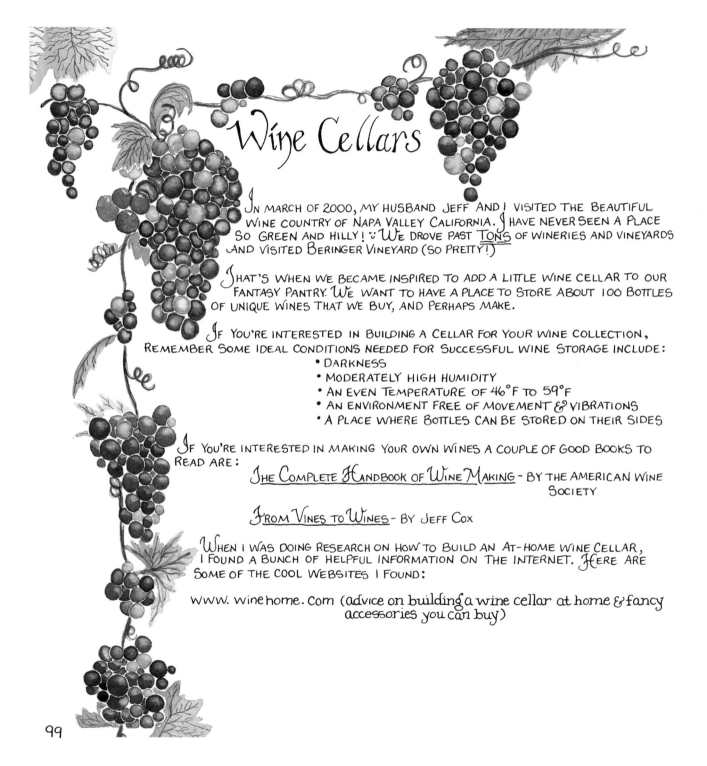

Wine Cellars

In March of 2000, my husband Jeff and I visited the beautiful wine country of Napa Valley California. I have never seen a place so green and hilly! ♥ We drove past TONS of wineries and vineyards and visited Beringer Vineyard (so pretty!)

That's when we became inspired to add a little wine cellar to our fantasy pantry. We want to have a place to store about 100 bottles of unique wines that we buy, and perhaps make.

If you're interested in building a cellar for your wine collection, remember some ideal conditions needed for successful wine storage include:

- Darkness
- Moderately high humidity
- An even temperature of 46°F to 59°F
- An environment free of movement & vibrations
- A place where bottles can be stored on their sides

If you're interested in making your own wines a couple of good books to read are:

The Complete Handbook of Wine Making - by the American Wine Society

From Vines to Wines - by Jeff Cox

When I was doing research on how to build an at-home wine cellar, I found a bunch of helpful information on the internet. Here are some of the cool websites I found:

www.winehome.com (advice on building a wine cellar at home & fancy accessories you can buy) www. stratsplace.com/rogov/art_build_cellar.html (a really good website about building your own cellar)

www. geocities.com/NapaValley/5996/index.html (free software for complete wine cellar management)

www. thewinecellar.ab.ca/cellarbuilder/default.html (unique wines to purchase for your collection)

www. winemine.com (how to make your own wines and what you'll need to do it)

www. winespectator.com (my favorite wine website. Includes cellaring tips, daily wine news, wines to try, wineries to visit, dining, and a wine gift shop.)

You may have heard about the many recent studies on the health benefits of MODERATE wine consumption.. (meaning 1 or 2 - 8oz glasses a day :) Here are a few tidbits that I've heard.
- Moderate wine consumption may help prevent heart disease and cancer.
- Substances in red wine may act as antioxidants.
- Moderate wine consumption may help prevent kidney stones.
- Moderate wine consumption may lower stress level.
- Moderate wine consumption may help reduce risk of stroke.

For more info. on this controversial subject you may want to read

Wine - Nutritional and Therapeutic Benefits - by The American Chemical Society. Edited by Robert J. McGorrin and Jane V. Leland.

"A book of verses underneath the bough, A Jug of Wine, a loaf of bread - and thou..."
Edward FitzGerald

little luxuries for
SPRING ~

♥ Reading books by Gladys Taber.

♥ Making gingham sachets to freshen closets.

♥ Decoupaging cute paper dolls and favorite quotes to a tea tray.

♥ Writing letters on pretty homemade stationary or cards.

♥ Browsing in variety stores, gift shops, hat stores and craft stores.

♥ Making a kite and flying it with your kids or your love. ☺

♥ Buying some new spring clothes and trying a new haircut.

♥ Using "Nantucket Briar" drawer liner paper by "Crabtree & Evelyn".

♥ Treating your mom to a champagne brunch on Mother's Day.

♥ Growing live grass baskets to give as special gifts on Easter.

♥ Going to the Door County Wisconsin Apple Blossom Festival.

♥ Making freshly squeezed orange juice & poppyseed muffins.

♥ Eating breakfast at an outdoor café with your best friend.

♥ Adding shutters and gingerbreading to your house.

♥ Buying yourself a new bottle of perfume and pink lipstick.

♥ Doing your spring cleaning and decorating with eyelet lace.

♥ Giving May baskets and watching Maypole dances.

♥ Riding on a carousel and sharing a cotton candy with your love.

♥ Watching a bird feeder outside your window.

♥ Going to art gallery openings.

♥ Running in the rain and splashing in puddles. Taking a nap afterwards.

♥ Pressing flowers and using pink notebooks.

little luxuries for

SUMMER

♥ Journaling on the beach and watching sailboats. Daydreaming.

♥ Building and using an outdoor shower in your own backyard.

♥ Hanging clothes and sheets on a clothesline to dry. So fresh!

♥ Double feature drive-in movies, building sandcastles, mint juleps.

♥ 4th of July parades, farmer's markets, Baking cherry pie, ✛ camping.

♥ Hosting a dinner party alfresco, or on a screened in porch.

♥ Using Italian blown glass swizzle sticks, dishes and glasses.

♥ Watching a production of a Shakespeare play in a park.

♥ Going to an amusement park that has BIG waterslides! Fun!

♥ Going to a Door County Wisconsin fish boil at a B & B Inn.

♥ Filling a hutch with beautiful vintage linens & antique lace.

♥ Putting white slipcovers on furniture for a beach house look.

♥ Going to Italian, Mexican, Indian, Polish and Oriental markets.

♥ Relaxing in a beach cabana all day with a good book.

♥ Going raspberry picking and then creating an excellent recipe
   for fresh raspberry pie with your best friend... Hi Sheri!

♥ Falling asleep in a big rope hammock while hubby mows the lawn

♥ Making homemade chocolate ice cream.

♥ Fireflies, dragonflies, butterflies & bees.

♥ Gardening: sunflowers & watermelons.

♥ European style marketing: Buy fresh
   flowers every week and fresh bread,
   meat and produce every day... Yum...

little luxuries for
AUTUMN~

♥ Making apple cider floats! Pour real cider over the best cinnamon ice cream you can find.

♥ Harvest grapevines and make homemade wreaths for Christmas gifts. Add bittersweet, moss, pinecones, & dried flowers.

♥ Going to an Italian style grape stomp and wine tasting.

♥ Going to an apple orchard festival. Pick apples and go on a hayride.

♥ Host a harvest party! Build a campfire, toast marshmallows...

♥ Flannel shirts, wool clogs, handmade sweaters, & fleece blankets.

♥ Pour cocoa over cinnamon toast for a cozy breakfast treat.

♥ Rustic decorating idea: Use a new rag rug in place of a tablecloth.

♥ Autumn decorations: rusty tin luminarias, patchwork quilts, quilted mug mats, a chunky pottery bowl filled with apples.

♥ Making soup and baking bread for supper. Mugs of coffee.

♥ Go on an Indian summer picnic and a hike in the woods.

♥ Creamy Chicken & wild rice stew, mulled cider, & candle light.

♥ Sitting outside and watching the birds & squirrels get ready for winter. Make pinecone birdfeeder by rolling a pinecone in peanut butter and birdseed. Hang on a tree.

♥ Waltzing by the light of a fireplace with your love.

♥ Pumpkin pie scented candles.

♥ A rustic cabin on a lake.

♥ Fondue for 2.

♥ Real maple syrup.

♥ Planting bulbs for Spring.

"Animal crackers, and cocoa to

little luxuries for
WINTER

♥ Velvet scarves and homemade Christmas gifts & Valentine cards.

♥ Bubble baths & breakfast in bed. Ahhh...

♥ Ice skating & boardgame parties with friends.

♥ Maple ice = maple syrup and freshly fallen snow. Fun for kids to make... an old time treat!

♥ Collecting antique and vintage Valentine cards.

♥ Going to a cozy tearoom on a weekly basis. Relax! ☺

♥ Burning plum pudding scented cake candles. Mmmm...

♥ Popcorn and cranberry garlands on outside trees for birds.

♥ Driving around your neighborhood to look at Christmas lights. Bring a thermos of cocoa & animal crackers.

♥ Snowmen, snow angels, snow forts, snowshoeing & skiing.

♥ Going to cut down your own Christmas tree & greenery.

♥ Special winter bedding including flannel sheet sets.

♥ Cranberry orange coffee cake, eggs, bacon, strong coffee & eggnog for Christmas morning breakfast.

♥ Start a snowglobe collection. Buy a new one every year. A wonderful heirloom!

♥ Trim a plaid flannel shirt with eyelet lace.

♥ Knitting mittens, slippers & sweaters.

♥ Cookie exchanges and progressive dinners.

♥ Romantic idea: Put a christmas tree in your bedroom & lights on your headboard

Can have what I please, I think I shall always insist upon these."

drink, that is the finest of

suppers, I think; When I'm grown up and

The End

"All that mankind has done, thought, gained or been: it is lying as in magic preservation in the pages of books." T. Carlyle